SHEFFIELD
IN THE SIXTIES

Peter Goodman

First published in Great Britain in 2001 by
The Breedon Books Publishing Company Limited
Breedon House, 3 The Parker Centre, Derby, DE21 4SZ.

ISBN 1 85983 235 0

Printed and bound by Butler & Tanner Ltd, Frome, Somerset
Jackets printing by GreenShires Ltd, Leicester

Contents

Introduction

BOOKS recalling a bygone era owe much to pictures taken at the time and can only come to life because a skilful photographer has used his or her expertise to capture a special moment.

This book, therefore, is a tribute to the Sheffield Newspapers photographic staff who worked for both *The Star* and *Sheffield Telegraph* in the Sixties.

Recognised nationally as one of the country's leading morning newspapers, the *Sheffield Telegraph*, which changed its name to *Morning Telegraph* in 1965, closed in 1986 but was reborn in 1989 as the thriving weekly newspaper it is today.

Both *The Star* and the *Telegraph*, in both its previous and present forms, can boast numerous awards over the years for the quality of their journalism and there have been many accolades, too, for the photographers on both papers whose work has received national recognition on many occasions.

The role of the newspaper photographer calls for tremendous resourcefulness and, as the pictures in the various chapters of this book show, the duties are many and varied. A 'snapper', for example, may have to brave blizzards to take a photograph of cars and buses stranded in deep snowdrifts – and an hour later he or she could be trying to persuade an unco-operative pop star to pose for a picture.

So my grateful thanks to all those photographers whose work is featured in this book and also to Angela Furniss and Nicola Ball from Sheffield Newspapers' photographic department for their much appreciated help and assistance.

PETER GOODMAN
SHEFFIELD
SUMMER 2001

Changing Face of Sheffield

Sheffield Corporation officials were not overstating the case when they proudly used the phrase "emerging city" in a special brochure produced to mark all the exciting new development taking place in the Sixties. New housing projects, roads, stores, hotels, markets and night spots were all part of soaring Sheffield as it met the challenge to compete with other growing cities and attract tourists.

Sheffield sparkled as never before on 8 December 1961, when the city's first Christmas Illuminations were switched on and the opening ceremony attracted massive crowds. This picture shows the scene on Fargate. It seems odd now to see traffic flowing through. The initial idea for the illuminations had come from John Goulden, then Director and General Manager of the *Sheffield Telegraph* and *Star*. Sheffield City Council and the Chamber of Trade gave it their full support.

Sheffield's Christmas lights dazzle Canadians

A TOWN in Alberta, Canada, has sent a business man to Sheffield on a fact-finding mission about the city's Christmas illuminations.

Man chosen by the Jasper Place Chamber of Commerce, is Mr. John Horan, aged 54.

He emigrated to Canada from the city 33 years ago and is now an established business man in Alberta.

Sheffield's first illuminations made such an impact that a town in Alberta, Canada, sent a representative over to pick up ideas for its own Christmas lights.

Below: A tableau showing the signs of the Zodiac in Fitzalan Square in 1962.

Fargate ablaze with lights in 1962.

The 1964 Christmas illuminations.

Huge crowds turned out for the 1968 illuminations switch-on.

Christmas 1969 and the Lord Mayor of Sheffield, Alderman Dan O'Neill, holds up the key to every home in Sheffield before handing it over to Father Christmas on his left.

The Lord Mayor, Alderman Dan O'Neill, switches on the Christmas tree lights at the Midland Station in 1969, watched by Kenneth Robinson, Assistant Station Manager, on his right and other officials and members of the public. Note the model train layout at the foot of the Christmas tree.

Sheffield's Park Hill Flats had no equal in the country, said Labour Party leader Hugh Gaitskell after performing the opening ceremony in 1961. The city, he added, had done a 'wonderful job'.

The flats, built by Sheffield's Public Works Department, were described by Coun Roy Hattersley, chairman of the Public Works Committee, as 'the most ambitious and most comprehensive housing scheme in Europe'.

The award-winning development attracted architects, planners and sociologists from all over the country – but there was criticism as well as praise.

The Town and Country Planning Association said the flats were 'huge rabbit warrens on steep slopes exposed to dirt, noise and smells'.

A view of the flats opened by Hugh Gaitskell.

A 1960 shot of Haymarket looking up towards Fitzalan Square. Davys Café, a popular meeting place for shoppers and office workers, is on the right, near the bus.

It was officially called the Castle Square Subway but everyone knew it as 'the Hole in the Road'.

And it was with some civic pride that it was declared open in November 1967. As the above picture shows, the ceremony, covered by a posse of journalists, took place in the subway itself.

Twenty-seven years later, the famous Hole was no longer a hole. Work began on filling it in early in 1994 and had been virtually completed by June of that year.

Work starts
on filling in the
Hole

The Moor, Sheffield, in 1961. It was described at the time as a "shopping centre in its own right, with new stores spelling prosperity." John Atkinson's new department store on The Moor had opened in 1960.

The new, illuminated Goodwin Fountain was switched on in November 1961.

High Street in 1961. The entrance to the Telegraph and Star building, now the Bradford and Bingley Building Society, can be clearly seen on the left.

January 1961, and drivers are having to get used to seeing a policeman on traffic duty at the junction of High Street and Fargate. The two islands are new and the policeman is waving traffic out of Fargate into High Street. It looks as though the bus, a 33 with Sheffield Lane Top on the front, is turning left up Church Street. This was the famous Cole's Corner where thousands of courting couples met over the years.

Angel Street, Sheffield, in 1962.
Peter Robinson's department store
is on the right of the picture and
Cockaynes store and the ABC
Cinema on the left-hand side of
Angel Street.

Barker's Pool in 1963. Glenn Ford is starring in *All This And Money Too* at the Gaumont and hungry cinemagoers can eat at the Green Room restaurant on the first floor.

The crowds are already starting to gather for the opening of Cole Bros new store in Barker's Pool in September 1963. The old store, at the junction of Fargate and High Street, had already been vacated and it meant that Cole's Corner, Sheffield's most popular rendezvous, had gone, at least in name.

Part of the large crowd waiting for the store to open.

The Lord Mayor, Alderman Isidore Lewis, cuts the tape to declare the store open.

Workmen on the roof of the old Cole Bros store in 1964 nearly a year after the company had moved out. No doubt they noticed the fine view down High Street before starting work.

Whoosh! The illuminated fountain outside the Midland Station was officially switched on in November 1964.

The River Don, high from winter rain, flows under Lady's Bridge, Sheffield, in February 1964.

A view of Castle Street, Sheffield, looking towards the new Castle Market buildings, in August 1964.

An atmospheric shot of the Wicker, Sheffield, on a dismal day in January 1964.

Sheffield Town Hall from Norfolk Street on a wet night in July 1965.

The junction of High Street and Angel Street in April 1965, not long before work started on the Castle Square subway complex

This photograph of Fargate shows how busy and bustling Sheffield city centre was in 1965.

The Hallam Tower Hotel, which opened in 1965, was nearly finished when this picture was taken in January of that year.

Chapel Walk, Sheffield, in October 1966.

Christmas shoppers in Waingate, Sheffield, in December 1969, looking from Castle Market towards Fitzalan Square. Note the sign on the street lamp for the Victoria Station, which closed in 1970.

Some parts of Sheffield were looking so untidy in the spring of 1969 that an Operation Springclean committee was set up. Members, recruited from all sections of city life including business, industry, the media and the Council, set about their work with immense enthusiasm and managed to carry the message to the public. The campaign was so successful that clean-up projects were still being undertaken later in the year.

As this picture shows, advertisements on bus sides helped to spread the message.

Youngsters were willing volunteers and Shirtclifffe Brook got the springclean treatment.

Even graveyards were tidied up and this project at St Thomas Church, Holywell Road, Brightside, was in the safe hands of fourth-formers from Hinde House Comprehensive School, Shiregreen, Sheffield.

This playground at Wybourn, Sheffield, was targeted as part of Operation Springclean.

May 1969, and Mrs E.Chadbourne, of Badger Road, Woodhouse, Sheffield, surveys a stream filled with rubbish at the bottom of her garden.

Tipping at Edmund Avenue, Bradway, Sheffield, attracted rats… and also the attention of the Springclean Committee.

Your Memories – Star Readers Recall the 60s

Sheffield Guides off To Norway

The smiles say it all. These Girl Guides and leaders can hardly contain their excitement as they pose for a picture at Sheffield Midland Station before heading off for Norway.

The year was 1960 and the Guides were from various groups throughout Sheffield. The picture comes from Jane Hurley, of Heeley, Sheffield, who is second from the left on the front row. She was Jane Newton then and just 15.

Woodseats Palace Cinema

Woodseats Palace Cinema, built in 1911, pictured in the Sixties. There's only one car to be seen on Chesterfield Road, which suggests that the road was much quieter then. Or was it a Sunday morning? Jane Hurley, of Heeley, Sheffield, thinks her father took the photograph.

Willie Socks It To Them!

Go, cat, go! Belting out a rock number is William Bembridge, of Crookes, Sheffield, who was then known as Willie of The Talismen.

The photograph was taken in 1963 at the Washington pub in Fitzwilliam Street, Sheffield.

Says William: "We never made it to the top but enjoyed ourselves just performing in pubs and clubs. The lad playing the guitar was 'Mad Rodger' and the drummer was called Dave. I have not seen either of them since the early Sixties."

The Day I Bumped Into Cliff Richard...

As Les Briddon says, it's not every day you go out for a stroll and bump into a pop star.

Les, of Hill Street, Sheffield, explains: "It happened to me in 1961. I was passing the St George's Hotel in Wellington, New Zealand, when Cliff Richard and the Shadows came out of the hotel.

"I asked Cliff if I could take his photo, he said 'yes' and then asked me, after I'd taken it, if it was okay.

"The funny thing about it all is that this same hotel was the main location for a Paul Newman film called *Until We Sail*. I have seen the film a few times and the hotel brings memories back of the day I met the now Sir Cliff."

Brightside – A Lovely, Friendly Community

Young and in love, Hazel Gee and Dennis Riley took these photographs of each other in their courting days.

Hazel, of Woodhouse, Sheffield, says: "We are still married after 36 years and often look through these old photos. These pictures were taken in 1963, on the old gun stand on Roman Ridge overlooking Brightside and the industrial valley which was quite smoky in those days but very clear now. The view then was spectacular, taking in Hadfields (now Meadowhall) and all the old steelworks. The house we bought in Tupton Street in 1975 is clearly visible to the right of Dennis and we lived in it until 1997 when we moved to Woodhouse.

"Our daughter and her husband and children live in the house now. We can't bear to part with it, as it is part of old Brightside. It was a lovely, friendly community and it was a pleasure to live there."

Fun On Blackpool's Golden Mile

Blackpool was THE mecca for South Yorkshire youngsters in the Sixties. It was a case of "be there or be square" and this group are definitely there and have the picture to prove it...

Mr D.Bradley, of Parson Cross, Sheffield, is on the far right of the top row and he says: "We were all 16-18 and regular dancers at the Roxy Ballroom at Page Hall, Sheffield. Most of us lived in the Firth Park area.

"We were enticed into a studio on the Golden Mile for this fun picture as I suspect none of us owned a camera at the time."

A Photographer At Ten...

It's easy to understand why Mrs Porter, of Prince of Wales Road, Sheffield, is proud of this Sixties photograph of her grandparents, Elsie and Harold Hickman.

She was ten when she took it, outside the guesthouse they were all staying in on Garfield Road, Scarborough.

Mrs Porter says: "Note the shape of the milk bottles at my gran's feet and how clean and litter free the road looks."

Beauties Spent The Night In Car

It's difficult to believe that these teenage beauties pictured looking spick and span on Cleethorpes seafront at 8.30am on a summer Sunday morning in 1964 had spent the night in a car! They shouldn't have been in Cleethorpes at all…

Says Lynn Bates (then Webber), at the time a 19-year-old shorthand typist at Thos W. Ward: " We were all staying at the Rotherham home of Marilyn Padley because her parents were away and suddenly decided we would go to Cleethorpes on the Saturday afternoon and sleep in the car overnight.

"It was a very daring thing to do in 1964 and none of our parents knew what we were about to do."

Marilyn was the only one who could drive and the car, a Vauxhall Velox with bench seats and column gear change, belonged to her father.

Lynn adds: "We had fish and chips and, as it began to get dark, Marilyn drove out of Cleethorpes until she saw a grassy place just off the main promenade. We decided it was a safe place to park the car and get some sleep.

"We were all extremely cold, cramped and had very little sleep with two of us in the back and two in the front. We were disturbed at 2am by some youths driving around our car and, because we were unable to lock the doors, we were all glad when it got light.

"At 7am we drove back into Cleethorpes to find a ladies toilet, had a wash, put some make-up on and the bouffant hairstyle was put back into place with the aid of a tailcomb and plenty of lacquer – no spray cans in those days.

"We fancied a cuppa and asked a chap who was opening up his camera shop on the main High Street if he knew any cafes. He did and asked if he could take our photograph.

"We returned to his camera shop later and this picture was the result.

"It was quite an adventure for four teenage girls back in 1964 but we never repeated it."

Lynn is third from the left on the picture and Marilyn Padley, the driver, is next to her on the far right.

The others are, from the left, Diane Salter, aged 19, a junior secretary at Thos W. Ward and next to her is her 18-year-old sister Gill, a hairdresser.

Marjorie And The Merry Widow

Sitting pretty on the far right of the picture is Marjorie Smith, of Norton Woodseats, Sheffield, during Sheffield Teachers Operatic Society's production of *The Merry Widow* at the Lyceum in November 1965.

She was Marjorie Wagland then and played the part of Valencienne.

Marjorie says: "They were very happy times to look back on and I still go to 'Teachers' rehearsals and help in any way I can. In fact, I was presented with my 50-year NODA medal in January 1999."

Happy Days At Butlins

Like thousands of other local teenagers at the time, Carol Pinder, of Dronfield, enjoyed holidays at Butlins where competitions of one kind or another were a big part of camp life.

Carol recalls: "This was my Jimi Hendrix period and I entered the Miss She competition for a joke. Needless to say, I wasn't quite what they had in mind!"

Dead Cool At Blackpool

It's 1963 and Jackie Harrison (right) and her friend Kath Warren (now Yeadon) are "trying to look dead cool all in black and with our Beatle haircuts while on holiday in swinging Blackpool."

Jackie, of North Anston, Sheffield, adds: "They were crazy times but we loved every minute of it."

Barbara Meets The Beatles!

Barbara Smith and her sisters Kathleen and Carol were the envy of their school pals in the Sixties. For dad was a commissionaire at Sheffield's City Hall where all the big pop stars of the day appeared.

It meant that the girls not only got to see their idols but also met many of them, including the Beatles, Rolling Stones, the Swinging Blue Jeans and the Dallas Boys.

Barbara says: "When we came out of school, we used to go into town for the first house at the City Hall. On one occasion, I was sitting on the stage before a show when the Beatles came in."

The sisters had their photograph taken with Adam Faith at the City Hall in the Sixties and again more than 30 years later when he appeared at the Lyceum.

Barbara, of Chapeltown, Sheffield, says: "He was pretty surprised when we showed him the old photograph."

The 60s… and Adam Faith signs autographs for Barbara Smith (far right) and her sisters Kathleen (next to Adam) and Carol.

More than 30 years later, the sisters meet Adam again outside Sheffield's Lyceum Theatre. Adam holds the Sixties photograph and the sisters (from the left) Kathleen, Barbara and Carol are all smiles.

Barbara meets Sixties heart-throb Eden Kane.

Barbara gets to grips with Ralph Ellis from the Swinging Blue Jeans.

Library Assistant Kay Booked For Wearing Hot Pants

As a 19-year-old library assistant in the late Sixties, Kay Waring always liked to look her best at work and keep up with the latest fashions.

And the day she appeared in hot pants on a mobile library unit, everyone remarked how nice she looked.

But her boss had different ideas. City librarian John Bebbington said at the time: "I have asked the staff not to wear this kind of garment at work because I don't think it is suitable."

The story made headline news in *The Star* and the paper also carried a photograph of Kay in her hotpants.

Kay, of Hacken-thorpe, Sheffield, also recalls the time in 1969 when boyfriend Richard Hardwick, now her husband, took her courting to Graves Park. He was wearing a suit and Kay, of course, was in her hotpants!

She says: "Richard and I are still very much together and love each other to bits."

Booked by her boss! Kay in her banned hotpants.

Boyfriend Richard went courting in his suit and tie.

Kay at Graves Park… again in hotpants.

Having A Ball At The Cutlers' Hall

Highlight of the year for employees of Thos W. Ward, Savile Street, Sheffield, was the company's Christmas Ball for all the staff. This happy picture was taken from the balcony of the Cutlers Hall.

Lynn Bates (then Lynn Webber) recalls some of the people on the photograph – herself, Barbara Fox and Elaine Fryer who all worked as shorthand typists in the Power Plant section with Mr Brown and Mr Frank Carnell as their managers; Stewart Ashton, Lynda Hunt and Barry Gall from other departments.

Side-Splitting Time For Cliff's Sheffield Fans

Cliff Richard fans Christine Palmer, her sister Brenda and friend Dorothy Grainger came up with a plan to meet their idol... they would get themselves purposely locked in the City Hall, Sheffield, after one of his concerts in the hope of finding his dressing room.

But it ended in failure and with Christine's tight skirt split more than it should have been!

Christine's sister Brenda Booth, of Ecclesfield, Sheffield, explains: "We were found and promptly ejected. Christine had split her tight skirt while trying to hide and had to walk home holding her skirt together with Dorothy and myself providing cover on either side of her."

Brenda and Christine lived opposite Dorothy and devised a code to make sure they would all be wearing the same kind of clothes when they went out, such as putting empty milk bottles in the window.

Christine Palmer (left) and Dorothy Grainger pictured in Belfast in 1960. They had gone with Dorothy's parents to see Dorothy's brother who had married an Irish girl.

Rocking With Ray In The Sixties

This publicity picture of Ray Gibson and the Wanderers taken in Graves Park, Sheffield, in 1961 will stir memories for fans of the local music scene in the Sixties. Standing left to right are Ray Gibson and Neil Broadbent and kneeling left to right are Ron Blythe, Gordon Porter, who supplied the photograph, and Cedric (bass guitar).

This 1960 membership pass for Club 60 belonged to Gordon Porter, who explains: "Club 60, situated in the cellars beneath the Acorn Inn, Shalesmoor, was Sheffield's own 'Cavern Club' and many top local bands used to appear there including the Cadillacs, Pete Fender and the Strollers, Dave Berry and the Cruisers and Ron Lindsay and the Coasters featuring the now legendary guitarist Frank White."

The Wanderers again, this time with new vocalist Barry Ford, pictured at the Shiregreen Hotel, one of the many venues for local pop groups. Says Gordon Porter: "We played all over Sheffield and South Yorkshire. They were great days."

Getting Married In The Sixties

This wedding photograph taken at Wadsley Bridge Church, Halifax Road, Sheffield on May 14 1960, was supplied by Mrs D. White, of Grenoside, Sheffield.

"I feel it reflects the spirit of the Sixties through the style of clothes," she says. The bride and groom are Marjorie Bark and George Evans, both of Parson Cross.

Up For The Cup In An Old Banger

1966 was a very special year, recalls Margaret Cutts, of Darnall, Sheffield.

England won the World Cup, Sheffield, which staged some of the matches, was buzzing with foreign visitors, and Sheffield Wednesday reached the FA Cup Final at Wembley.

She says: "My husband Trevor and his pals painted up an old van and set off for Wembley. The fact that only two of them had tickets for the match didn't matter.

"It seemed like the whole of Sheffield was outside the Town Hall to cheer Wednesday back home, even though they had lost. It was a brilliant atmosphere.

"I remember singing and chanting football songs in the pubs and bopping at the Locarno with my friend Julia. It definitely was the Swinging Sixties!"

Trevor Cutts and his pals painted up an old van before setting off for Wembley.

All The Fun Of The Fair – In Silly Hats!

This picture of Sheila Tidy (right) and her friend Sandra enjoying themselves at a fair in Farm Grounds, Granville Road, Sheffield, actually appeared in *The Star* in 1961.

Sheila explains: "It was taken by a *Star* photographer and I still have the original. The silly hats we were wearing were made out of crepe paper."

When Sheila unearthed this photograph and realised she hadn't been in contact with Sandra for many years, she succeeded in tracing her to Leeds. The two of them have spoken on the phone and are planning to get together again to talk about the old days.

What Dreams Are Made Of – But It's Real For Carole

When Carole Commander looks back on the Sixties, she remembers a star spangled sequence of events that most pop-mad teenage girls could only dream about...

It all started in the late Fifties when she was 16-year-old Carole Ward. International singing star Paul Anka, himself only 16 at the time, was touring Britain and due to play the City Hall, Sheffield.

Because she was a great fan, Carole, then studying on a secretarial course, wrote to him for an autographed photo. Paul replied and after a further exchange of letters invited Carole to meet him when he came to Sheffield!

Says Carole: "He invited me to have lunch with him at the Grand Hotel, where he was staying, and I was so

The fateful photograph... Carole with Eddie Cochran in February 1960, just a few weeks before his death. The picture was taken in the Green Room restaurant situated above the Gaumont in Barker's Pool, Sheffield.

Carole helps Paul Anka sort out his fan mail backstage at the Hippodrome Theatre, Manchester.

excited. Here was I about to have lunch with one of the best-known pop stars and songwriters in the world.

"We met and chatted over lunch, which I think was fish. I was a little nervous at first but I soon felt relaxed because Paul was such a down-to-earth person. It was then he invited me to run his fan club in England."

She eventually became his international fan club president and secretary, producing monthly newsletters and magazines and meeting up with him every time he came to England.

He also kept Carole informed of all the latest news from his travels around the world.

As the fan club grew in the late Fifties and early Sixties, it made more sense for it to be based in London. But Carole wanted to stay in Sheffield where her roots and all her friends were.

"Rather reluctantly, I decided to give the job up. It was beginning to take up so much time and I didn't really want to move to London. But working for Paul was absolutely fabulous while it lasted. In those days, it was what dreams were made of," Carole adds.

The young secretary met a host of top stars including Buddy Holly, the Everly Brothers, Cliff Richard and the Shadows, Billy Fury and Gene Vincent in the late Fifties and Sixties but she had one particular favourite… Eddie Cochran.

And in a strange twist of fate, she met and interviewed him in Sheffield only a few weeks before he was tragically killed in a car crash at Chippenham, Wiltshire, in April 1960.

Because of her enthusiasm and knowledge of the pop scene, *The Star's Top Stars* pop music magazine regularly invited her to interview and write about the big names when they were in Sheffield and she jumped at the chance when Cochran came to the Gaumont Theatre.

Cochran had been appearing at Bristol Hippodrome the night before his death. The tragedy left the

Carole backstage at the City Hall, Sheffield, with Phil and Don, the Everly Brothers, in April 1960.

pop world and Cochran's fans worldwide stunned. Only 21, he had already recorded three mega hits, *Summertime Blues*, *Three Steps to Heaven* and *C'mon Everybody*.

Carole decided to send a sympathy card and letter to Eddie's grieving family in America and it was to lead to a remarkable friendship which goes on to this day.

To Carole's surprise, his mum and dad wrote back to thank her and enclosed a photograph of Eddie.

The letters and phone calls have continued over the years and, after Eddie's parents died, his sister Gloria kept the contact going. She died in 1998 and her son now keeps in touch. The family have also sent Carole gifts over the years, including one of Eddie's cravats.

Carole, who now lives in Stannington, Sheffield, says: "There are so many wonderful memories from the Sixties and it was a privilege to be a teenager growing up during such an exciting decade."

Sheffield Group On Six-Five Special

One of the most popular and best known local groups of the Sixties was the Greycats Rhythm Group and if you weren't in the queue by 6.30pm whenever they were playing, you didn't get a seat!

The group had national exposure when they appeared on the *Six Five Special* television show and also at the State Kilburn in London with Pete Murray.

Locally, they played at Sheffield's Empire Theatre, the Gaumont Cinema, the Mojo Club, the Locarno on London Road and many of the clubs in the South Yorkshire region.

The Greycats at the Sicey Hotel, Shiregreen, Sheffield, in the Sixties.

The Greycats also featured in a Sheffield *Top 10 Star Show* at the City Hall in 1963 presented by the Stringfellow Brothers.

The group was third on stage, just before Joe Cocker, then known as Vance Arnold and the Avengers. Top of the bill that night was Dave Berry and the Cruisers.

Drummer Dennis Loveday still has a drum skin signed by Jackie Collins, Wee Willie Harris and Mickey Most.

His wife Elaine says: "The group have stayed together as friends and still meet for social and musical get togethers. They bring their instruments along and

Drummer Dennis Loveday – his drum skins were signed by the famous.

even now there's still the magic of a group who were and are very professional and give a great sound."

Jean said "Hello" to the Sixties

As a Sheffield teenager in the Sixties, Jean Senior never stopped saying 'hello' to people – and she loved every minute of it!

For Jean was a telephone operator at GPO headquarters on Flat Street and the job suited her bubbly personality down to the ground.

Jean and Keith on honeymoon at Babbacombe, Devon.

She was working there when STD (Subscriber Trunk Dialling) was introduced and it led to her going out 'on loan' to telephone exchanges in different parts of the country.

In her spare time, Jean took full advantage of all Sheffield had to offer adventurous teenagers in the Sixties… shopping at the new stores, dancing to the latest music at clubs such as the Mojo and the Black Cat and ten-pin bowling at Intake.

She has particularly fond memories of a rock club held at Frecheville Church Hall and recalls seeing Long John Baldry there.

Says Jean: "Sheffield was an exciting place in the Sixties and it was absolutely fabulous to be a teenager. There was so much going on and we didn't like to think we were missing a minute of it."

Wedding bells rang for Jean in May 1969, when she married Keith Havenhand.

A Sunday afternoon at Clumber Park for Jean and Keith in July 1966.

High Winds and Low Temperatures

Hurricane Terror Hits Sheffield And South Yorkshire

Few Sheffield and South Yorkshire people over 45 will need reminding about the most vicious winds they are ever likely to experience...

The hurricane of February 1962 was truly terrifying. It killed four people, injured many others and destroyed thousands of homes, schools and other property.

In scenes reminiscent of the Blitz, a state of emergency was declared in the city and emergency centres were set up throughout the area to give shelter to the homeless.

As in the Blitz, the city's people and emergency services worked tirelessly and courageously to help and comfort the injured and restore some kind of order from the chaos.

The Star's front page on Black Friday, 16 February 1962.

The scene on Northern Avenue, Arbourthorne, Sheffield. The hurricane attracted national attention and on the left of the picture a television cameraman can be seen filming the destruction.

Dr Charles Hill, Minister for Housing and Local Government, visited the city to see the damage and talk to the victims. Here he meets George Duke and his family, of Hollinsend Road, Intake, Sheffield, at the Burngreave Vestry Hall reception centre.

The hurricane brought awful tragedies. A 17-year-old died when the roof of this house on Colwall Street, Sheffield, collapsed on him.

This wall on Shoreham Street, near Bramall Lane football ground, was flattened by the wind.

George Brown, Deputy Leader of the Labour Party, inspects the damage at Attercliffe, Sheffield, with the Lord Mayor, Alderman J.W. Sterland, and Alderman Mrs Grace Tebbutt, leader of the Council.

Even The Beer Froze in 1963!

Apart from 1947, the dreadful winter of 1962-63 was the worst of the 20th century.

It was so cold – 20 degrees of frost (Fahrenheit) were recorded on 21 January 1963 – that even diesel oil and beer froze.

Sprouts at Sheffield's Parkway Market were 'more like balls of concrete', cabbages like bricks and a cat, frozen to the roof of a house by its tail, couldn't move and had to be rescued by firemen.

Trains were marooned in deep drifts, it was chaos on the roads, a Hull barge couldn't leave Sheffield Basin for a week because of thick ice, emergency standpipes had to be used because the water supply froze, homes were blacked out by power cuts and there were severe gas shortages because of demand exceeding supply.

This snow-shifting scene was commonplace in the winter of 1963.

The sub zero temperatures didn't stop
the fun for these children from
Broomhill, Sheffield.

Skating on thin ice? Not these young ladies pictured at Whiteley Woods, Sheffield.

As these pictures taken at Bramall Lane show, there was little football played during the deep freeze of '63, despite valiant efforts to clear pitches of snow and ice.

Havoc in Matlock. Flooding caused chaos in December 1965 and this shot of Bakewell Road shows water lapping up to shop windows and doors.

Causeway Lane, Matlock, on 10 December 1965.

Not a good day for listening to the band – Matlock town centre gardens in December 1965.

This car and van stuck in deep floodwater on Rotherham Road at Templeborough in December 1965 have both been abandoned.

Pop Goes the Sixties

"You've never had it so good," proclaimed Prime Minister Harold Macmillan in the late Fifties.

He might very well have been talking about the advent of the Sixties pop scene, arguably the most effervescent explosion of music we are ever likely to see.

It is significant that an unashamedly nostalgic road show, the Solid Silver 60s, has been playing to packed houses across the UK since 1985 and its popularity shows no sign of waning.

Fittingly, its 2001 production includes Sheffield's own Dave Berry in its line-up, as well as Peter Noone, Dave Dee, Dozy, Beaky, Mick and Tich, and Wayne Fontana.

Sheffield attracted all the big stars throughout the Sixties and the following photographs take us back in time to that spirited, swinging decade.

Adam Faith slicks his hair into place before facing his fans at Sheffield City Hall in February 1960. In December 1959, he had topped the charts with *What Do You Want?* and was number one again a month after this picture was taken with *Poor Me*. Poor Me, indeed! Young Adam was well on the way to his first million…

Heartthrob David Whitfield set the girls swooning when he visited the offices of *The Star* and *Telegraph* in 1964. Most of the tenor's hits, such as *The Book* and *Answer Me*, were recorded in the Fifties and he was the first British singer to win a gold disc, for *Cara Mia*, in 1954. David was only 54 when he died in 1980.

Sandie Shaw pictured at Sheffield's Grosvenor Hotel in 1967. She had huge hits with *Always Something There to Remind Me* in 1964, *Long Live Love* in 1965 and *Puppet on a String* in 1967.

The year is 1963 and Brenda Lee poses for Sheffield Newspapers cameraman Geoff Tyrer at the City Hall. Her big hit was *I'm Sorry* but we were far from sorry to see her in Sheffield.

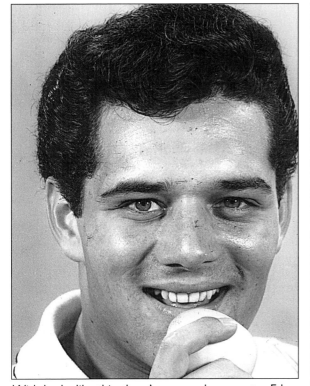

With looks like this, there's no wonder pop star Eden Kane turned many a girl's head in the Sixties. A public relations company promoting the benefits of eating apples for healthy white teeth issued this picture. As the PR people said at the time, you'd expect a guy with a name like Eden to have a thing about apples!

Georgie Fame admires the Sheffield skyline in 1969. A year earlier, he had hit the heights with *Bonnie and Clyde*.

Before appearing on stage at the Gaumont Cinema, Sheffield, in 1965, the Batchelors surprised projectionist Derrick Goodison by presenting him with a silver cigarette box and a badge to mark his 25 years with the cinema.

Billy Fury snapped in Sheffield while preparing to do some snapping of his own... Because of his gold lamé suits and sexy gyrations, Fury was often described as the 'English Elvis Presley'.

The smile suggests that singer Michael Holliday was pleased to be in Sheffield in 1962. In January 1960, he had topped the British charts with *Starry Eyed*.

Just look at the admiring glances from fans as pianist Russ Conway tours *The Star* and *Telegraph* Outdoor Living and Gardens Exhibition held in the grounds of Sheffield's Kenwood Hotel in 1964.

Do you remember when things were really humming? Chubby Checker puts trainee twisters through their paces in 1962 when Britain's biggest dance craze of the Sixties was at its height.

Chubby's first record, *The Twist*, came out in 1960 and the follow-up, *Let's Twist Again*, a year later. The twist is still popular today, testing the knee joints and lung power of young and old alike at Christmas parties and wedding receptions.

And here's the man who started it all. Chubby relaxes in his dressing room at the City Hall during the interval of his show in September 1962.

Matt Monro died, aged 54, in 1985 but the voice lives on through such unforgettably beautiful ballads as *Portrait of My Love*, *Softly As I Leave You*, *Walk Away*, *Born Free* and *Yesterday*.

He is pictured here in 1968 after opening Sheffield Chrysanthemum Society's show at the City Hall.

Acker Bilk was no stranger to Sheffield and South Yorkshire in the Sixties and the trad jazz giant topped the bill at the Sheffield University Students Union ball in June 1963. His *Stranger on The Shore* was the UK's best-selling single in 1962.

You were meant for me, everybody tells me so, says two-year-old Joanne Smith as wacky pop star Freddie Garrity from Freddie and The Dreamers opens a new Tesco supermarket at Darnall in 1968.

Sheffield's Shining Star Of The Pop World

Way ahead of its time and highly regarded as one of the best pop music supplements in the country, *The Star's Top Stars Special* was a must for Sheffield and South Yorkshire teenagers in the Sixties.

Mums and dads read it, too, and much of its success was due to the hard work and vision of Roy Shepherd, a *Star* journalist with a phenomenal knowledge of the local and national pop scene.

Top Stars Special was very much Roy's baby and his sheer enthusiasm for Sixties music shone out of every page.

The stars liked it too and often took a copy away with them when they visited Sheffield.

Sadly, Roy died in 1974 but his contribution to local journalism through *Top Stars Special* has a special place in *The Star's* history.

Joe Brown (doesn't he look young?) enjoys his copy of *Top Stars Special* during a visit to Sheffield in February 1963. He's too modest to be looking at his own picture, which is on the back page.

Swinging! Jazz singer George Melly found *Top Stars Special* very much to his taste when he came to Sheffield in 1963.

Top Stars Special regularly handed out awards to pop stars, with readers voting to decide the winners. Tom Jones was top male vocalist in 1967 and received his award at the Gaumont Theatre, Sheffield, where he was appearing. This was Tom's first visit to Sheffield.

A *Top Stars Special* editorial planning session at *The Star* in 1963. Roy Shepherd is seated in the middle.

Tuning up in Sheffield in October 1962, are the Temperance Seven, top of the UK charts at the end of April 1961, with *You're Driving Me Crazy*.

Big O, American singing star Roy Orbison, appeared at Sheffield's Gaumont Theatre in 1965 and Sheffield Newspapers photographer Dennis Richmond was there to record the event.

Oh, Pretty Woman and *It's Over* had both been chart toppers for Orbison in 1964.

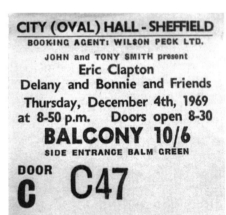

As these City Hall admission tickets show, Sheffield attracted quality musicians in the Sixties.

Mick Jagger in the Sixties (far left). The Rolling Stones never seemed to be away from the Sheffield City Hall in those days. And they were back at Sheffield Arena 30 years later.

Sheffield's own Dave Berry first exploded on to the pop scene in the Sixties and has been a splendid ambassador for the city ever since. It has always surprised, and delighted, him that so many of the stars from that decade are still playing today.

"We thought we'd just have three or four good years but here we are, still playing", Dave said in the late Nineties.

Dave, whose big hits included *The Crying Game* and *Little Things*, not only knew but played with the big stars from the Sixties. He is still great friends with many of them.

Nothing ruffled cool Dave's feathers, not even the flock of pigeons released when he opened a new boutique in Sheffield in April 1967. The Birdcage boutique was at Cockayne's store and the white bits floating down from the sky are not snowflakes… just pigeon feathers.

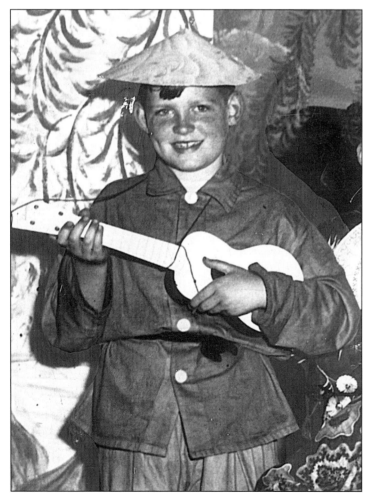

1967 – and by now he is Joe Cocker and his Grease Band.

Here's another young Sheffield lad who has spread the city's name across the world. Joe Cocker, guitar in hand, was 11 at the time. In the early Sixties he called himself Vance Arnold and showed the first real signs of the stardom to come when he played Sheffield's Esquire Club (now the Leadmill) on Leadmill Road in 1962.

Joe enjoys his copy of *The Star* in 1994.

Probably Joe's proudest ever moment – receiving an honorary doctorate from Sheffield Hallam University in 1994, with his brother Victor and father Harold. It was for his services to the international music industry and for publicising the dangers of drug dependency.

Club 60, in the cellars of the Acorn Inn on Shalesmoor, Sheffield, was a popular haunt for teenagers in the Sixties.

Frank White was something of a Sheffield legend in the Sixties and still is. He pioneered the use of the double-neck guitar in this country, played with Dave Berry's Cruisers in the early Sixties and had a Friday night residency at the Pheasant, Sheffield Lane Top, for 18 years. The sessions drew fans from all over the country. Frank, highly regarded as one of the UK's top guitar players, is still delighting his legion of fans with performances at clubs and pubs.

This picture of Frank (bottom centre) and his Katters was taken in 1966. The Katters are (left to right) Alan Wood, Dave Green and Gerry Wigley.

Recognise the one on the left? Along with his brother, Geoff, he was showing entrepreneurial flair as long ago as 1964 when this picture was taken. Peter Stringfellow, once described as Sheffield's most flamboyant son, is now regarded as the world's number-one nightclub boss.

It all started going right in the early Sixties when the brothers opened their first nightclub, The Black Cat, in a church hall on City Road, Sheffield. It attracted big names such as Gene Vincent, The Hollies and Dave Berry.

The next venture, the Blue Moon Club near The Wicker, had Rod Stewart, then a singer with the Long John Baldrey Band, and The Kinks among its illustrious visitors.

The Mojo Club, off Barnsley Road, Pitsmoor, was the biggest and best known enterprise, with Stevie Wonder, The Who, The Temptations, Ike and Tina Turner and The Move all enjoying top billing. Elton John, then known as Reg Dwight, was also there. Promoter Peter also brought Mick Jagger and the Stones to Sheffield City Hall in the early Sixties (for £120) and The Beatles to the Azena Ballroom in Gleadless in 1963.

The church hall where it all started. In 1994, Peter Stringfellow came back to Sheffield to trace his pop roots.

Sheffield-born Reginald Dixon, the famous Blackpool Tower organist who made 3,000 radio appearances, announced his retirement in 1969.

Reginald Dixon on a visit to Sheffield to see his parents.

We will probably never know what George Harrison was looking at and why he was standing on a chair at Sheffield City Hall when the Beatles came to town in November 1963. Three weeks after the picture was taken, the Beatles were at number one with *She Loves You* and finished the year with another chart topper *I Want to Hold Your Hand.*

John Lennon in a Sheffield taxi in 1965.

Paul McCartney with one of the Moody Blues at Park Hall Country Club, Spinkhill, near Sheffield, in December 1965.

(Left) Praise indeed for the Beatles in 1964.

YOUTHS ARE POOR COPY OF BEATLES

THE BEATLES are a shining example of how hair should be kept clean and tidy—but Sheffield youths who try to copy them only succeed in having long, dirty, unkempt hair, Sheffield Education Committee was told yesterday.

The attack on the city's youths came during a debate on the annual report of the principal school medical officer, Dr. Llywelyn Roberts, in which reference was made to dirty heads and hair.

Coun. E. Tindall told the committee of a recent occasion when he walked behind a group of young people along Chapel Walk. "I could not tell whether they were male or female," he said.

"I just could not imagine their heads or hair were clean. For years we have been told the incidence of nits among girls was due to their long hair, and I wish parents who have sons would be a little more careful about how they look after their hair."

Mike *Come Outside* Sarne on the stairway to success at Sheffield Gaumont in September 1963.

Gene Pitney in Sheffield. *A Town Without Pity*, *24 Hours From Tulsa* and *Something's Gotten Hold of Me* were all hits.

Who can forget Tiny Tim and his version of *Tiptoe Through The Tulips*? He didn't have to tiptoe through any tulips when he planted a tree in the Peace Gardens in November 1969 as part of Sheffield's Plant-A-Tree fortnight.

Vince Hill was always a popular visitor to Sheffield and here he is in 1969 signing autographs at a Variety Club of Great Britain function.

Jimmy Crawford was the first in a long line of Sheffield pop stars to have a hit record. The former Davy United draughtsman gave the city something to sing about in 1961 with *I Love How You Love Me*.

Who's this fiddling about in Sheffield in 1966? Jimmy Tarbuck went on to prove that he had more than one string to his bow.

Sheffield Mourns Pop Star's Tragic Death

It didn't quite fit the image of a typical Sixties pop star when Dickie Valentine, heart-throb crooner with a string of hits to his name, asked if he could be baptised at Sheffield Cathedral.

At the time, he was playing Buttons in the 1968 production of *Cinderella* at the Lyceum. Canon Dennis McKee, then precentor at the Cathedral, was only too happy to carry out the baptism because Dickie had already established close links with Sheffield and always went out of his way to help local charities whenever he appeared in our area.

Just three years later, a grieving Canon McKee was conducting his funeral service after the pop star had been tragically killed in a car accident in Wales. He was 41. His worldwide fan club was devastated, as were his many friends in show business.

When he died, his great mate Frankie Vaughan was appearing at Sheffield's Fiesta Club. A few days earlier the two of them had had dinner together.

Dickie Valentine (far right) in pantomime at the Lyceum.

A shocked Frankie said at the time: "We were laughing and joking and making all sorts of plans for the future. He was the sweetest person in the world. I never heard him talk badly of anyone."

Canon Mckee echoed Frankie's sentiments. "He was a good man and we are all lucky to have known such a person," he said.

Dickie met his second wife, singer Wendy Wayne, in Sheffield in 1968 when they were both playing in pantomime at the Lyceum.

Thirty years after his death, Dickie's big hit, *Finger of Suspicion*, is still heard on the radio from time to time, a reminder not only of the Fifties and Sixties pop scene but also of a star whose warmth endeared him to Sheffield.

Dickie was always keen to help local charities, particularly the Variety Club of Great Britain Sheffield which raised money to buy sunshine coaches for use by underprivileged children.

Dickie's great friend, Frankie Vaughan, was also a regular visitor to Sheffield and in 1971 received a surprise Christmas card from *The Star* Women's Circle, a thriving club for the newspaper's women readers in the Sixties and Seventies. It was presented to him by two members of *The Star's* Promotions and Publicity Department.

In one Sixties pantomime in Sheffield, Dickie's children Kim, aged ten, and nine-year-old Richard, went on stage near the end of the show to join him in a song.

Dickie Valentine dies in blazing car

SINGING star Dickie Valentine, who shot to the top of the show-business tree in a classic rags-to-riches story, died today in a car crash in South Wales.

Two other men, his drummer and pianist, also died when the car, owned by Mr. Valentine, crashed into a bridge parapet and burst into flames.

It took police several hours to identify the bodies, which were badly burned, but late this afternoon they confirmed that 41-year-old Valentine, his drummer, Dave Pearson, and pianist Sid Boatmen had died in the blazing wreck.

The crash occurred at the tiny village of Glangrwyney, on the A40 Brecon-Abergavenny road.

CALL-BOY

Mr. Valentine had been appearing this week at a Caerphilly club. An official said today his shows there had been a huge success.

It was at first feared that Dickie Valentine's manager, Eddie Jarratt,

Drummer and pianist are other victims of crash

was one of the victims, and police were trying to trace him.

Mr. Jarrett was booked into the Park Hotel, Cardiff, last night, but did not turn up, and it is believed he left Cardiff to arrange further bookings in West Wales.

Dickie Valentine's climb to the top of the show-biz tree was a classic rags-to-riches story.

His father was a lorry driver, and his first introduction to the stage was as a 14-year-old page boy at the Palace Theatre, Manchester. When his father's work brought him to London, Dickie also trans-

ferred as page boy to the Palladium.

He was sacked for being cheeky and moved on ', running errands for the stars. But he returned to the Palladium in 1956—as top of the bill.

SWITCH

In 1949 Dickie made his debut with the Ted Heath band, and stayed with the band until 1954, by which time he was top of the pops on both records and 'ele vision.

His television shows as

well as his records jumped into the top ten, but a few years later his popularity fell.

He gradually changed his image from pure por to becoming an entertainer including impressions and comedy in his act. He returned to television qv years ago with his own ITV programme

His marriage to Eliza beth Flynn, a professional ice skater, was dissolved i 1967 afer 13 years. The had two children, Richard and Kim. Three years ago Dickie, who is 41, marrie actress Wendy Wayne

The Star's front page story announcing Dickie's death.

Leisure and Entertainment

Lord Mayor Skates Through Official Duties

No one was suggesting the Lord Mayor of Sheffield was failing to keep up with his civic duties when, in 1965, they told him to get his skates on…

Alderman Jack Worrall was only too pleased to oblige. After all, Sheffield had a new ice rink and he had the privilege of opening it.

The kids loved the Silver Blades, as did the mums and dads, and the new venue quickly became a family crowd puller.

After opening the Silver Blades, Ald Worrall took to the ice with Carol Windebank.

The Birmingham Barrel Jumping team gave a breathtaking demonstration at the opening ceremony.

Floorshow at Sheffield's Cavendish Club in 1967.

Dancing championships at the Top Rank, Sheffield, in 1969.

Working Men's Clubs have always been popular in our part of the world and in the Sixties many of them staged top quality "turns", particularly at week-ends.

But the clubs are best known for their top quality beer and company and this picture, taken at a working men's club at Birdwell, Barnsley, in 1962 is testament to that.

Amusement arcades were taking on a smart new look in the Sixties. This one, the Golden City, was on Eyre Street, Sheffield.

The Gay Tyrolese Dancers appeared at the City Hall in October 1967, and gave an impromptu show for Sheffield Newspapers photographer George Heppinstall.

Remember go-go dancing? These three girls were the finalists in a go-go competition at the Penny Farthing disco in Sheffield. The competition combined fashion consciousness and dancing ability.

Left to right are: Winner Betty Nixon, Avril Cochrane (third) and runner-up Christine Hague.

As Max Bygraves used to say, "they've turned our local Palais into a bowling alley and things aint what they used to be." Certainly in the Sixties, tenpin bowling alleys, many of them former cinemas, were springing up all over the place. These enthusiasts are pictured at the CBC Bowl at Intake, Sheffield, in 1967.

The setting is Universal Bowling on Queen's Road, Sheffield, in 1965.

Sixties singer Sheila Buxton cut the ribbon when the Fairlanes Alley, Firth Park, Sheffield, opened in 1963.

Ready for the opening of the Fairlanes Alley, Firth Park, in 1963...

Ken – A Legend In Everyone's Lunchtime!

A councillor started one of Sheffield's best known and longest running institutions when, in 1967, he suggested that office and shop workers sitting around eating their lunches in the city centre should have some music to listen to.

Blind organist Ken Outram was hired to provide it in the City Hall Ballroom and his music was so infectious that people were soon up on their feet. The office and shop workers found that dancing the lunchtime away was better therapy than dancing the night away and so began a tradition which lives on to this day.

Ken, now 74, became the original legend in his own and also other people's lunchtime and some of those Sixties dancers are still tripping the light fantastic at the Tuesday and Thurday lunchtime sessions.

(Left) Ken at the organ with his former guide dog Heidi.

(Below) This picture of Ken (on stage) playing for dancing was taken in the City Hall Ballroom in the late Sixties.

Singer Ronnie Hilton (left) and comedian Ted Rogers (right) starred in *Humpty Dumpty* at the Lyceum Theatre, Sheffield, in December 1964.

The campaign to save Sheffield's Lyceum Theatre from demolition started in 1969. This picture was taken in the Sixties.

Final Flicker Before The Lights Went Out

As new night spots opened in the Sixties, it was perhaps inevitable that something had to give on the entertainments scene and several cinemas felt the cold draught of closure.

The Adelphi at Attercliffe, a favourite haunt of generations of Sheffield Eastenders, closed in October 1967.

Four years earlier, the Hippodrome, in Cambridge Street, Sheffield, which had started life as a theatre in 1907, met the same fate, as did the Woodseats Palace in 1961.

Another 1961 closure was the Cinema House in Barkers Pool, Sheffield.

Bingo took over when the Manor Cinema shut in 1963 but it eventually became a supermarket.

The Wicker Cinema closed after a bad fire in 1967 but re-opened as the Studio 7 in 1968. It finally met its end in 1987.

The Woodseats Palace, which closed in 1961. *Konga* was the film being shown when this picture was taken.

Hot stuff at the Wicker Cinema, badly damaged by a fire in 1967. The film billed in this 1962 photograph is *Ritual of Love* – 'The primitive passions of the world's dark and distant places.' On with it is an X-film, *Woman in the Window*.

The Wicker Cinema just before it re-opened as the Studio 7 in 1968.

No shortage of customers here for the Hippodrome on Cambridge Street which closed in 1963.

A 1961 victim was the Cinema House in Barkers Pool. Two years earlier, you could have watched Gary Cooper in *North-West Mounted Police*.

(Above) The Adelphi at Attercliffe just after its closure in 1967.

Thriving when this photograph was taken in 1965 was the ABC Cinema on Angel Street, Sheffield. The feature film is *The Hill*, starring Sean Connery, Harry Andrews and Michael Redgrave. Coming soon is Elvis Presley in *Tickle Me*. Wonder if they managed to illuminate the 'A' in ABC before Elvis arrived?

Television

The Goggle Box That Changed Our Lives...

Television had been installed in many Sheffield and South Yorkshire homes in the middle and late Fifties but, as the Sixties dawned, it was still something of a novelty. And it was, of course, very much a black and white affair.

Not that it mattered. The fact that new technology had brought moving pictures into our living rooms (we didn't call them lounges then) was mind boggling in itself and no one cared that the screen was colourless.

Viewers were spellbound and thought the output was well worth the £4 licence (it increased to £5 in 1965).

One programme in particular caught our imagination at the start of the decade but few of us realised then that it would run... and run... and run... and run...

"Every front door hides a story," said the publicity blurb for the new twice-weekly serial starting on 9 December 1960.

It certainly did. And still does all these years later.

Coronation Street was born....

Was there life before *Coronation Street*? Television personality Russell Harty summed it all up when he said: "There was life before the Street but it didn't add up to much..."

Without a doubt, television was changing our lives. How on earth had we managed without it?

Sunday Night at the London Palladium paraded the world's top variety stars before our very eyes and dramas such as the *Forsyte Saga* gripped the nation, so much so that some churches in our region changed the times of their Sunday night services to avoid a clash.

Quiz shows such as *Double Your*

There aren't many houses here without a television aerial. The goggle box has arrived...

Money and *Take Your Pick* ("Open the box" we roared to contestants from our fireside chairs) were an instantly popular form of family entertainment because we all felt a sense of involvement.

The youngsters had never had it so good. *Juke Box Jury, Top of The Pops, Ready Steady Go...* all the latest smash hits tumbled noisily out of the little walnut box in the corner. And while most grandparents – and some mums and dads come to that – frowned, the kids clicked their fingers to the beat, swung and swayed their hips and wondered how the older generation could be so square.

For football followers, 22 August 1964, was a time of awe and wonder – the first *Match of The Day*, on BBC 2.

Unless you were an Arsenal fan, that is. Beaten 3-2 by Liverpool, Gunners' supporters were probably

Early *Coronation Street*. The smile on Hilda Ogden's face suggests she's happy with the Sixties prices at the corner shop... 2s 6d for beef steak in gravy (just over 12p in today's money!).

Martha Longhurst,

not impressed that Roger Hunt's first goal for Liverpool had made television history.

They called the telly the goggle box in those days. It was a frighteningly accurate description because that's what everyone did, night after night. Goggle...

We loved every flicker. And no one seemed to notice very much when, in August 1962, *The Star* published an article about the Great Britain National Radio and Television Exhibition being held at Earls Court.

It said that colour television was to be demonstrated at the exhibition for the first time.

It was 1967 before colour came to Sheffield. The city's Grand Hotel proudly announced that it was to buy a colour set for its lounge and the news was sufficiently important to guarantee a headline in *The Star* that night.

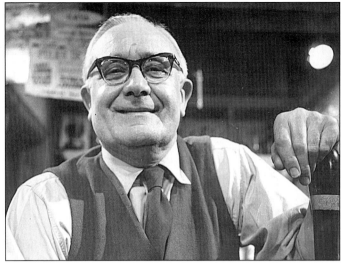

Stalwarts of the *Street* in the Sixties... Jack Walker and Ena Sharples.

Elsie Tanner (Pat Phoenix) was the *Street's* first 'hussy' but we always knew that a soft heart lay behind that apparently hard exterior. That's why we all loved her. She was in Sheffield in 1962 to open Parkhill Wine Stores.

Pat met up with Frankenstein and his Monsters, a successful Sheffield group, at Handsworth Working Men's Club, Sheffield, in 1966.

Pat at Sheffield Lyceum in 1969.

This was a 1964 scene from the 100th episode of *Z-Cars*, a BBC police drama series involving crews Z-Victor 1 and 2. Standing by for action while a roof chase is under way are (from left): PC David Graham (Colin Welland), PC Herbert Lynch (James Ellis), PC Jock Weir (Joseph Brady) and PC 'Fancy' Smith (Brian Blessed).

What a shower! Note comedian Dick Emery (top row, right) in this 1960 photograph of the cast from *The Army Game*.

Crossroads, with Meg Mortimer (Noele Gordon) as the motel owner, started in 1964 and this 1967 shot shows her (third from the left) with the rest of the cast.

Football was a television favourite in the Sixties and the ABC TV cameras were at Hillsborough in September 1966, for the Wednesday v United derby game. The crowd was 43,557 and the score 2-2. Both sides finished mid table that season, with United just ahead with 42 points from 42 games, one more point than Wednesday.

COLOUR STAYS 'IN THE AIR'

By ALAN MORRIS

Our Radio Correspondent

DESPITE the B.B.C.'s demonstrations of colour, experts still have not produced an economic British tube or decided on which of the two available systems we should adopt.

the time comes you should make sure that only skilled TV technicians fix them.

Having conquered the outdoors radio market, transistors, the tiny germanium replacements for bulky valves, are now breaking into the

and the user does not need any extra radio licence.

Signs of a price war at the show are confined to salesmen of "pocket" radios.

The lowest tag reads "10 Gns" and there is one set

Colour television, which arrived in 1967, was still some way off when this headline appeared in *The Star* on 21 August 1962.

A South Yorkshire actress found fame and became a household name in 1964. Doncaster-born Diana Rigg starred as Emma Peel in the television series *The Avengers*, taking over from Honor Blackman as John Steed's assistant.

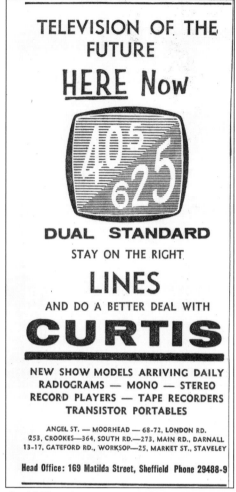

A 1962 advertisement from *The Star* heralds the introduction of 625-lines television sets.

Health, Fitness and Fashion

U.K. HEART GRAFT PATIENT 'FIT,' SAYS SURGEON

BRITAIN'S first heart transplant patient was today described as "fit" after a successful operation at the National Heart Hospital in London yesterday.

The Sixties was a pioneering decade and none more so than in the field of health.

An important medical breakthrough came in 1967 when Dr Christian Barnard performed the world's first human heart transplant in South Africa. The patient died but the operation paved the way for the many successful transplants carried out since.

A South Yorkshire nurse had a part to play in Britain's first heart transplant at the National Heart Hospital in London in May 1968.

Doncaster-born Sister Isobel Curry was in charge of the operating theatre nursing staff who assisted at the five-hour operation. She told a press conference at the time: "We had done two operations that morning, both on children, and about 11am we heard that a heart transplant was in the offing and that a possible donor had been located.

"I immediately prepared the theatres and all the various other jobs which have to be done. This included keeping a lot of curious members of the staff away. Once they knew this was coming up, they all wanted to have a look."

The recipient, Frederick West, aged 45, died two weeks after the transplant.

In 1963, an operation on a 37-year-old Sheffield bachelor, salesman Peter Lucas, of Sky Edge Road, Sheffield, made surgical history.

He received a kidney from a dead man at Leeds General Infirmary and it was believed to be the first time the transplant had been successfully performed.

A world first for a Sheffield patient.

Kidney graft for city man

OPERATION A SUCCESS

A KIDNEY from a dead man has been successfully transplanted during a six-hour operation into a 37-year-old Sheffield bachelor.

The operation has made surgical history. It is believed to be the first time it has been successfully performed in the world.

Health and fitness was an important part of many local lifestyles in the Sixties. Proving in 1962 that there can be gain without pain (judging by the smiles on their faces) are these ladies from Barnsley Telephone Exchange. Photographer Roy Sabine, now living happily in retirement in Southern Ireland, took the picture.

1965… and members of a keep-fit class at St Mary's Community Centre, Bramall Lane, Sheffield, go through their paces.

Chilblains galore—but girls stay slaves to fashion

WOMEN in Sheffield prefer to suffer for the sake of fashion. They shiver in nylons and high heeled shoes, crippled by chilblains, to satisfy their fashion - conscious pride.

The winter of 1963 was one of the coldest of the century and women in Sheffield came under fire from a doctor for putting fashion before common sense and good health.

The doctor said that they preferred to shiver in nylons and high-heeled shoes and be crippled by chilblains just to satisfy their fashion conscious pride. He advised them to wear slacks during the cold spell.

A reporter from *The Star* carried out some research in the city centre for an hour during the peak shopping period and found only two women with slacks on.

Health and fitness was a priority for many women in the Sixties – and so was beauty. A new beauty counter was set up at the High Street, Sheffield, store of Boots in 1969 and customers were invited to try the make-up products. In charge of the counter was Mrs Margaret Peters, of Birley, Sheffield.

Eve of Roma girls at work at Walsh's store, Sheffield, in 1969. Letizia Pacini (right) applies eye make-up to Dilva Miotto (seated) as store consultant Mrs Hadfield looks on.

A Max Factor promotional picture from 1964. The caption said: "A little girl's present to mummy on Christmas morning – a Creme Puff – brings happy smiles."

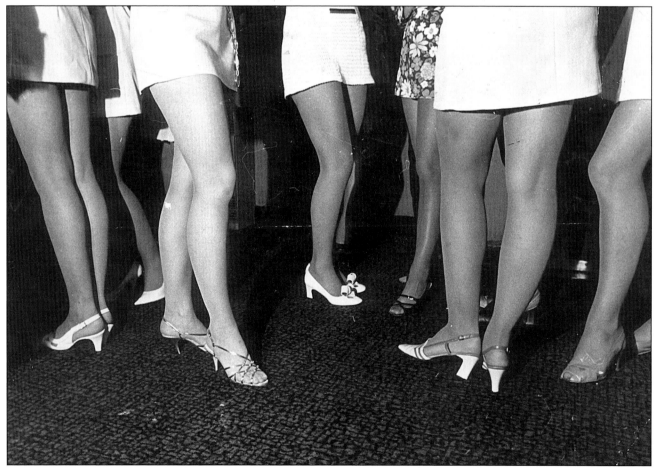

Sheffield legs on view in 1969. The picture was taken to accompany a feature on mini skirts in the *Sheffield Morning Telegraph*.

These models look as though they are waiting for take-off to another planet. The picture was taken in Sheffield in October 1962, but the venue is unknown.

Mini skirts in the grounds of Sheffield Cathedral in 1966.

Casual wear being modelled at a 1963 Sheffield and Ecclesall Co-op store fashion show.

A model shows off a Big Ben zipper jacket at a 1962 wool fashion show at Walsh's store, Sheffield. Also in the picture is James Norbury who compered the show and designed the clothes.

Capes were popular and fashionable during the bitterly cold, record-breaking winter of 1963. This canary yellow number, modelled at Roberts Bros store, Sheffield, cost nine guineas and the hat was 27s 11d.

This pink Chanel suit with floral Tricel blouse, modelled at a Fashion Rendezvous show in Sheffield in 1963, would have set you back nine guineas.

This model turned a few heads in the middle of Sheffield in 1962.

Male and female hairstyles from the Sixties.

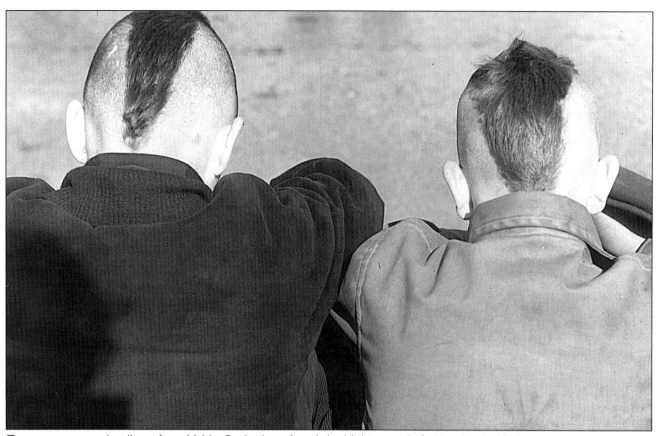

Two anonymous schoolboys from Maltby, Rotherham, found the Mohican style fashionable in 1960.

Men's suits normally came with a waistcoat in the Sixties.

Shock for stores as topless dresses prove a sell-out

THE few Sheffield region shops that stocked tople[ss] dresses as a gimmick have sold out and a[re ta]king orders for more come through quickly [to meet] the demand.

[The] general feeling [is that wom]en are buying th[em as a lau]gh, and only the [odd cus]t[omer] have the courag[e to] wear one.

[At] Elizabeth Gowns[,] Road, Sheffield, [and Ma]rche in Donca[ster's] Place, where top[less dresses w]ere on display [, pu]blic interest has [been high.]

[B]uyers at both bo[utiques bought] [d]resses each [day . . .] . . . and have [come] with requests

Topless dresses, or "shock frocks" as they were known, sold well in Sheffield initially but the market soon went flat, so to speak. The few shops that did sell them thought women were buying them as a gimmick and not to actually wear them.

Looking the picture of health, Miss World, Lesley Langley, signs autographs at Cockaynes store, Sheffield, in March 1966.

These legs, belonging to Rotherham mum and beauty queen Nina Scott, were voted the loveliest in the country in 1968 – and immediately insured for a million dollars by a company who had lined up a programme of personal appearances to publicise stockings. And two-year-old son Richard couldn't have been more proud...

On the Roads

The driver of a pay-as-you-enter bus sorts through his change in July 1969. This would have been the conductor's job before one-man buses came along.

It's Goodbye To Trams... and Bus Conductors

On the roads, the Sixties saw the introduction in Sheffield of one-man, pay-as-you-enter buses, parking meters, traffic wardens and the breathalyser.

The first one-man bus ran on the Sheffield-Huddersfield route in March 1967, followed in September, 69, by the first one-man operated double decker on seven routes.

It seems odd that today's teenagers probably won't remember bus conductors.

The city's first four traffic wardens were on the streets in 1966, six years after London. They were, said the Chief Constable, "ambassadors for the police force" and their main job was "to be helpful and show goodwill towards the motorist."

Parking meters arrived in 90 city centre streets in November 1967, a month after the breathalyser.

We said an emotional farewell to the trams on a very wet night in October 1960. They had been with us through two world wars and, when they went, it was like saying goodbye to old friends.

Sheffield's Leadmill Road bus depot looking all spick and span on the day it opened in July 1963. The chairs at the front were for guests attending the opening ceremony.

Unlucky for some! Traffic warden number 13 in action in Campo Lane, Sheffield, on 13 November 1967, just after the introduction of parking meters.

Many motorists were caught out on Bank Holidays during the early days of the parking meters, assuming they still had to pay. Susan Bright, of High Green, Sheffield, feeds sixpence into this meter on Good Friday 1969.

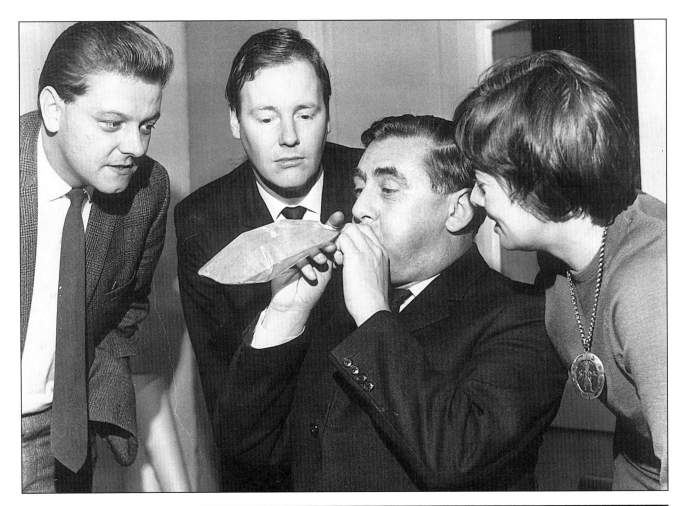

Goodness knows why anyone should think journalists are ideal subjects to test new breathalyser equipment! These four sober news hounds are from the editorial staff of the then *Morning Telegraph*. Watching Peter Bloxham blowing into the bag in November 1967 are, from left to right, Mike Holloway, Eric Walker and Dinah Maiden.

Some pubs had re-action meters in the pre-breathalyser days and you could check the speed of your response in a simulated emergency stop. The machine also gave your braking distance.

Always a popular Derbyshire beauty spot at holiday time, it wasn't really a surprise to see so much traffic congestion at the 'Surprise' view on the Hathersage road at Easter 1969.

A reminder of what cars looked like in the Sixties... and also a reminder of how busy it was at Ladybower Reservoir in 1968.

Many Sheffielders didn't realise how fond they had become of the trams until they lost them. This picture shows car 122 at Millhouses terminus in April 1960.

The last tram to run, car 510, was accorded a special place at Crich Tramway Museum where it was eventually restored to pristine condition.

All aboard for Blackpool North Station in the summer of 1968? Not quite – this old Blackpool tram, pictured at Crich Tramway Museum, Derbyshire, is miles from the sea.

A Rotherham trolley bus in November 1964.

A snowy day in Sheffield in January 1968. This picture of the bus station, with the Midland Station to the left in the background, was taken from the GPO sorting office in Pond Street.

Days Out and Holidays

Big Day Out Had Family Appeal

One of Sheffield's top annual events throughout the Sixties was the *Telegraph* and *Star* Gala. Normally held at Oaks Park, Norton, it attracted thousands of people and the wide range of activities gave it family appeal. All it needed for the perfect day out was good weather.

This selection of pictures takes us back to 1965...

All the fun of the fair...

They say that an apple a day keeps the doctor away so I'll have two, thank you very much. But this little girl has a sticky time ahead of her.

Eyes down and look in 1965- style. The players are using bottle tops to cover the called numbers on the bingo boards.

Wonder why they call them dodgems when all most kids want to do is bump the car in front?

Thirteen-year-old twins Patricia and Carol Ellis enjoy a high-speed ride on the Cyclone. Mark Bright, aged ten, sits between them, seemingly holding on for dear life.

A large crowd watching the entertainment at the 1960 *Telegraph* and *Star* Gala. This event was held at the Granville Road grounds.

Hold that tiger! The annual Sheffield Show was another great family day out in the Sixties and the Lord Mayor, Ald Jim Sterland, known as 'Sunny Jim' because of his pleasant nature, took time out in 1961 to meet the Yorks and Lancs Regiment's mascot.

Eva Schell, a visitor from Germany, isn't quite sure what to make of it all.

Who said the sun always shone in the Sixties? There are plenty of umbrellas up at the 1961 Sheffield Show as the entertainment gets under way.

Wow! A huge hydraulic excavator on one of the trade stands captures the attention of these two boys at the 1964 Sheffield Show.

An anti-tank gun causes interest at the 1965 Sheffield Show.

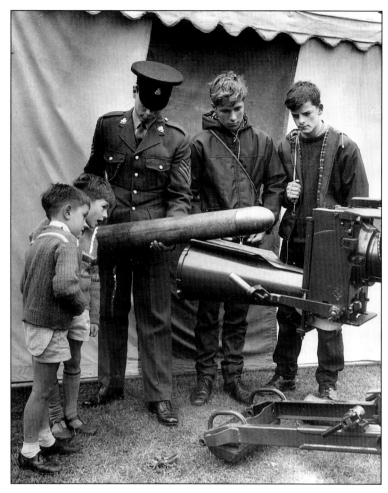

Jumping for joy at the 1967 Sheffield Show is Diana Clarke, of Arbourthorne, Sheffield. Private John Hogg of the Yorkshire Brigade is right up there with her, making sure she comes to no harm.

The 1967 Sheffield Show was opened by the Lord Mayor, Ald Harold Lambert, whose friendly approach to civic duties won him many admirers during his year of office.

With him as he inspects exhibits in the floral art section are the Lady Mayoress, Mrs J. Lambert, and Coun Bill Owen, chairman of the Show Committee.

The year is 1962 and there's a buzz around Pond Street bus station as these seaside-bound holiday makers queue for their coaches.

A children's playground at Attercliffe, Sheffield, in 1962.

Peace, perfect peace, at Crookes Valley Park, Sheffield, in 1966 when warm autumn sunshine attracted these bowls spectators.

A Whit Bank Holiday scene in Sheffield in 1968.

Military Tattoos attracted big crowds and ready to take part in a 1962 event at Sheffield Owlerton Stadium are members of the 'D' Rotherham Company of the Hallamshire Battalion.

Grub's up for these Scouts from the 4th St Paul's Troop, Sheffield, at the 1965 Scouts Jamboree at Chatsworth. The sausages are sizzling but there's no sign of the beans. Perhaps they are being cooked on another fire.

Putting the garden in order at John Eaton's Almshouses, Bunting Nook, Sheffield, was the task for these bob-a-jobbers in 1965. Sheffield's Lord Mayor, Ald Smith prepares them for the "off."

The triumph on the faces of these Rotherham cubs is unmistakable after they had built their own soap box car in 1962.

It's not clear whether these scouts from the 3rd Brampton, Chesterfield, troop are intending to use this hot water for washing in or to make tea. Whatever, they're having a great time at the 1965 Chatsworth Jamboree.

Sheffield's Peace Gardens live up to their name in May 1969.

High Hazels Park, Sheffield, in 1967.

Children from the Norfolk Park area of Sheffield take part in a play project in July 1967.

1963 Spring sunshine in Firth Park, Sheffield.

The Duke of Edinburgh visits
Old Hall School, Rotherham, in
May 1967... and it's raining.

Royal Visitors

A Red-Carpet Welcome For Our Raining Royals!

Our area gave a typically warm welcome to Royal visitors in the Sixties but the same couldn't always be said of the weather.

The Duke of Edinburgh suffered more than most. Whenever he came to our region, it was usually raining or snowing. He seemed to spend the decade sheltering under an umbrella.

It proved beyond doubt that he was no fair-weather Royal…

The Duke of Edinburgh in Sheffield in February 1969… and it's snowing.

The Duke came to open new buildings at Sheffield University in November 1961… and he's looking up at something. Rain clouds? Or the sun?

Princess Margaret and Lord Snowdon with the Mayoress of Chesterfield, Mrs E.B.Robinson in May 1963.

Princess Margaret attended the rehallowing of Sheffield Cathedral's extensions in November 1966, and Mr A.Bailey, the architect, showed her a model of the new buildings. Looking on are the Very Rev. Ivan D.Neill, Provost of Sheffield, and Mr J.B.Radley, a chorister who made the model.

Princess Margaret meets some of the guests at the Cathedral.

The Queen Mother opened Hyde Park Flats in June 1966 and attracted a large crowd of well wishers. Many tenants lined the balconies of the flats to get a bird's eye view.

During the same visit to Sheffield, the Queen Mother also opened Sheffield University's Arts Tower, describing it as the "power house of the University from where the batteries of young men and women will be charged to enable them to go out into the world to be leaders of new generations."

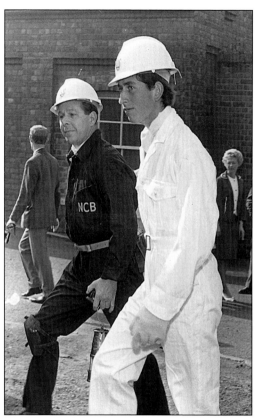

The Duke of Edinburgh almost back into daylight after going underground at Bevercotes Colliery in July 1967. He is pictured with George Edwards, the colliery's general manager.

Like father, like son. Prince Charles visited Welbeck Colliery in June 1968.

The Queen at Matlock Station in May 1968, accompanied by the Lord Lieutenant, Sir Ian Walker-Okeover. A contingent of the Leicestershire and Derbyshire Yeomanry stand to attention.

The Queen steps off the Royal Train on her arrival at Grindleford Station in October 1969. She is received by the Duke of Devonshire (far left) and Mr C.L.Burton, Area Manager, British Railways, Buxton.

Shall I or shan't I? Princess Margaret looks tempted by the food stall during a visit to Edale in May 1969.

Harry Heap – King of the Cartoonists

A skilful cartoonist whose clever drawings reflected the life of Sheffield and South Yorkshire over a 40-year period retired in 1965 and, sadly, died three years later.

Harry Heap was famous in the days before picture power transformed newspapers, joining *The Star* in 1928 and drawing 10,000 cartoons for three generations of readers.

His work covered most aspects of city life including council meetings, dinners, presentations and shows but he was probably best known for his sports cartoons.

He would normally set the scene for Saturday's local football games with a cartoon in *The Star* on Friday evenings. It would preview the South Yorkshire action, particularly Wednesday and United.

His drawings of players in action, and the goals, in the *Green 'Un* sports paper the following day were a revelation. Even last minute goals were often included, an incredible achievement considering that he had to have his illustration ready to send to the print room only minutes after the final whistle had blown.

For many years, Harry used a cartoon character called Alf, a typical football fan who loved to sound off about the local teams. Comparing him to a ventriloquist's dummy, his inventor once said: "You can get away with saying rude things in a cartoon and I use Alf as my mouthpiece."

It was fitting that when Harry died, many of the people he had sketched during his lifetime were at his funeral.

Harry on retirement day.

A typical Friday night cartoon from the Sixties.

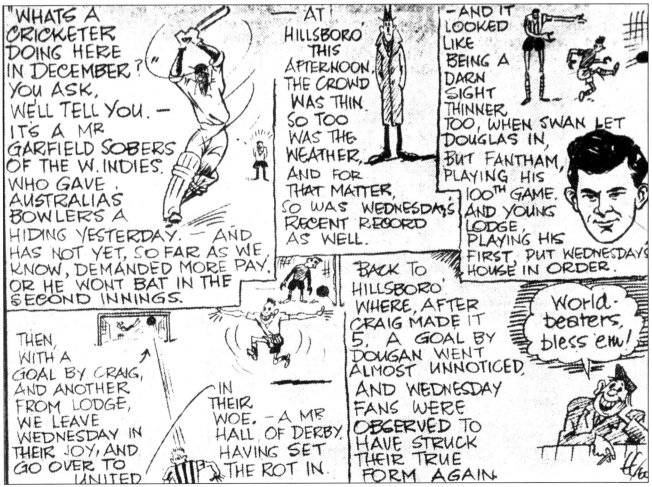

A 1960 drawing produced for Saturday night's *Green 'Un* sports paper.

The Political Scene

Labour Lose Control Of Sheffield For The First Time In 35 Years

It was certainly a political sensation when the Tories captured Sheffield City Council in May 1968.

The Labour stronghold was overturned after 35 years when the Conservatives scraped home with a 56-52 majority.

They had just a year in power – Labour took control again in May 1969, with a 57-51 majority. It prompted Ald Ron Ironmonger, Labour's leader, to say: "We are certainly wiser men after a year in opposition."

The Tories were able to claim one record while they were in power – one Council meeting debating spending cuts in July 1968 went on for an incredible 13 hours 14 minutes! It ended just after 4am.

This historic picture was taken in May 1968 after the Conservatives captured control of Sheffield City Council.

The new group met in the Town Hall to hear leader Alderman Harold Hebblethwaite (seated second from left) read a telegram of congratulations from Prime Minister Ted Heath.

Also seated from left are Ald S.K.Arnold, Ald D.J.O'Neill, Coun T.W.Lambert and Coun Miss Pat Santhouse.

Prime Minister Harold Macmillan enjoys a joke with guests at a reception held in Sheffield's Grand Hotel in 1961.

Ted Heath checks the time during a visit to Sheffield in March 1965. Four months later, he was to take over as leader of the Conservative Party from Sir Alec Douglas-Home.

Harold Wilson in Sheffield in June 1963 without his Gannex coat!

He had then been leader of the Labour Party for six months, taking over from Hugh Gaitskell after his death in January 1963. The following year, Wilson was Prime Minister after leading Labour to victory in the General Election.

When Tragedy Struck

Pit Disaster Stuns Local Community

A pit disaster at Silverwood Colliery, Thrybergh, near Rotherham, in February 1966, devastated the local community and shocked our region to the core.

It was a chilling reminder that, despite the high standards of safety introduced over the years, collieries could still be dangerous places.

An empty paddy train ran into the back of another carrying 40 miners to the pit face. The men were thrown out on impact and nine died, with a further 21 injured.

The accident happened 2,500 feet below ground and the men were just 500 yards from their destination when tragedy struck.

PIT DISASTER: 9 DIE, 21 HURT

Hospital ready for injured

First arrival at Rotherham Hospital, Doncaster Gate, was 53-year-old Jack Nettleship, of Sandy Drive, Ravenfield, who had both feet severed.

By Star Reporting Team John Piper, Tom Geeson, Eric Towner and Frank Baldock

NINE miners were killed and 21 injured today when two paddy mail trains collided half a mile underground at

News of the tragedy breaks on the front page of *The Star*.

Angels of Mercy... these three nursing sisters, Kathleen Payne on the left, Diane Adsetts and Mary Parton, went underground to treat the injured.

Colleagues wait at the pithead for news of survivors.

Shaken and injured miners are helped by their workmates.

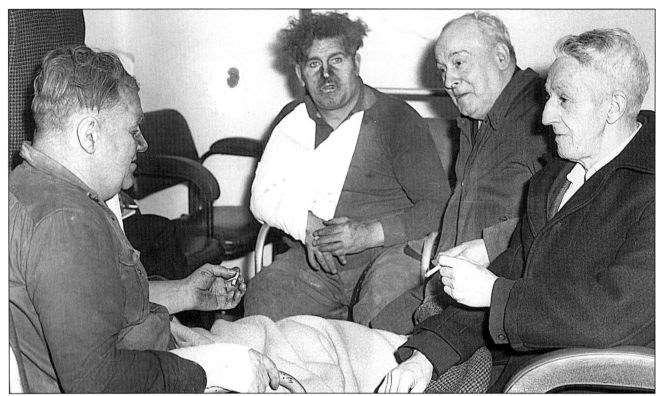

Casualties pictured after treatment at Rotherham Doncaster Gate Hospital. Left to right are Leslie France, Luke Brennan, John Hallsworth and Ernest Devine.

Four Die At Cortonwood Colliery

Four miners lost their lives after an escape of methane gas at Cortonwood Colliery, Wombwell, Barnsley, in 1961. So much gas was released when a roof collapsed that it stopped fresh air coming into the area where the men were working.

Pit deputy Joe Gibbons and overman John Pattison bravely made ten attempts in two hours to rescue their colleagues but were pushed back by the gas.

Cortonwood Colliery on the day of the disaster.

BREAK IN FLOOR RELEASED DEATH FUMES-MANAGER

Inquest told how gas 'flooded' pit

The inquest was told that 750,000 cubic feet of gas escaped into the workings.

WITHIN two hours of a break in the floor at Cortonwood Colliery, where four men died in June, 750,000 cubic feet of gas escaped into the workings, it was stated at the inquest at Wath today.

"In actual fact the quantity of gas released was such that it stopped fresh air coming up to the district and pushed back 250 to 300 yards along the main gate," said Mr. Edwin H. Lunness, the pit manager.

Railway Guard Jumps For His Life

A goods train driver leapt from his engine seconds before it crashed into another goods train on the main Sheffield to Chinley line at Totley, Sheffield, in June 1966. He was treated in hospital for face cuts and allowed home. The guard on the other train also jumped from his brake van when he saw the goods train bearing down on it.

About 60 men using giant mobile cranes worked throughout the night to try and clear the line.

The wreckage after two goods trains crashed.

Chambermaid Twins Leap 70ft From Hotel Window

Twins Sandra and Molly Wilson were both seriously injured after jumping 70 feet to escape a fire which broke out in the early hours at the Grand Hotel, Sheffield, in 1966.

The 21-year-old chambermaids leapt from their smoke-filled bedroom as fire engulfed the top floor and landed on a low flat roof which broke their fall.

Sandra had fractured arms and legs and spinal injuries and Molly fractured legs and spinal injuries.

Sandra had reached the fire escape at one point but went back to look for her sister.

Other staff and guests in their night clothes were led to safety down staircases.

Singing star Ronnie Carroll was also staying at the hotel and he sprained an ankle while rushing from his bedroom.

Twins Sandra and Molly Wilson jumped 70 feet to escape a fire which broke out at the Grand Hotel.

Singer Ronnie Carroll was staying at the Grand Hotel when fire broke out.

The weight of ice brought the Emley Moor television mast crashing down in March 1969. No one was injured but the village chapel was damaged and Yorkshire Television transmissions to our area blacked out.

Worldwide Sorrow For Student Neil

The biggest rescue attempt in potholing history became an international story in 1959 when 20-year-old university student Neil Moss was trapped in Peak Cavern, Castleton.

A 44-hour fight to save him failed despite the heroic efforts of the rescue team and his body had to be left in the cavern.

His father told the inquest that he knew where his son's body lay and he was perfectly prepared to let it rest there.

But the terrible tragedy didn't stop adventurous potholers pitting their wits against some of Derbyshire's most challenging underground caves in the Sixties.

Several found themselves in difficulties and were thankful for the help of the rescue services.

The awesome Giant's Hole at Castleton, Derbyshire, proved particularly daunting and, in March 1968, student Peter Rose was trapped for eight hours in an 18-inch high passageway leading to the Hole 300 feet underground.

Peter, secretary of the Sheffield College of Technology Speleological Society, had

Peter Rose is rescued after his eight-hour ordeal and a warm drink helps to revive him. He was treated at Sheffield Royal Infirmary for exposure and a hand injury.

already crawled through it once but went back to help three female potholers.

He became wedged by his hips and chest and Derbyshire Cave Rescue teams, police and firemen worked throughout the night to rescue him.

Canadian student Donna Carr sustained skull injuries after an accident in Giant's Hole in 1965.

Her father flew to Britain from Canada as soon as he heard the news and was relieved to find her alive.

Injured potholer Charlie Carson, fastened to a stretcher and wrapped in polythene, is carried to a waiting ambulance after being rescued from Giant's Hole, Castleton, in November 1966.

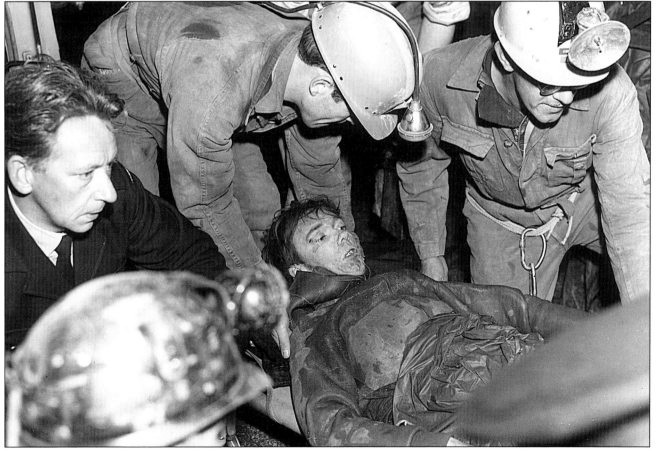

Sheffield University student Henry Mares is assisted on to a stretcher after being rescued from the Maskill mine, near Castleton, in October 1966.

Sitting up in her hospital bed, Donna Carr, with father Don, holds flowers sent by the team who rescued her.

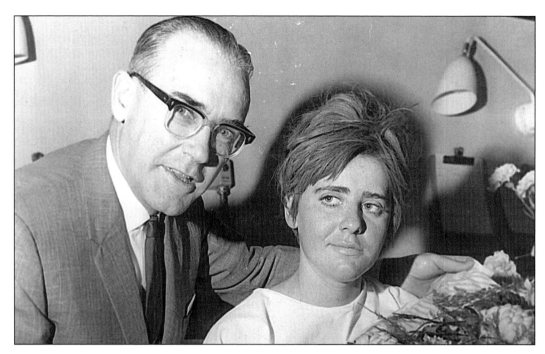

And Before Tragedy Struck... President Kennedy At Chatsworth

The peaceful June afternoon President John Kennedy spent at Chatsworth, Derbyshire, in 1963 now stands in stark contrast to the horror that was to engulf the world just five months later.

It was one of the best- kept secrets for ages when the sun-tanned President arrived by helicopter to visit the grave of his sister Kathleen in Edensor churchyard. Killed in an air crash in 1948, she was the widow of the Marquess of Hartington, the Duke of Devonshire's older brother, who had lost his life in Italy during the Second World War.

He stood quietly by the grave before going on to visit the Duke and Duchess of Devonshire at nearby Chatsworth House.

The President arrives at Chatsworth.

Sister Kathleen's grave. Her epitaph reads: "Joy she gave. Joy she has found."

Such was the shock when President Kennedy was assassinated in November 1963 that anyone a teenager or older at the time can remember exactly where they were and what they were doing when they heard the news.

The President's younger brother Bobby also visited Chatsworth in January 1965. He, too, was to die at the hands of an assassin, in 1968.

Sporting Days

A Decade Of Ups And Downs

Sheffield's football fans were tasting success and buzzing with anticipation at the start of the decade. Both sides had made a stirring start to the Sixties. In the 1960-61 season, Wednesday finished runners-up to Spurs in the top division (then Division One) and United were celebrating promotion from Division Two.

So, with both clubs in the top flight, hopes were high, especially when United finished a very respectable fifth in the following 1961-62 season with Wednesday sixth just a point behind.

But by the time the Seventies dawned, both sides had dropped out of the top division. United were relegated in 1967-68 with 32 points from 42 games and Wednesday came down in 69-70, with just 25 points from 42 games. They had scored 40 goals all season, conceded 71 and finished bottom.

United were promoted again in season 1970-71.

There were mixed fortunes for our other local teams in the Sixties. Rotherham dropped from Division Two in 1967-68, finishing second from bottom.

Barnsley finished bottom of Division Three in 1964-65 and were relegated but managed to claw their way back in 1967-68.

Chesterfield were relegated from Division Three in the 1961-62 season and spent the decade in Division Four until 1969-70 when they won promotion back to Three.

Doncaster won promotion from Division Four in 65-66, were relegated in 1966-67 and then promoted again in 1968-69.

This was the Wednesday team in December 1960, the season they finished runners-up to Spurs in the top division. Back row (left to right): Swan, Johnson, Springett, Young, Kay, Megson. Front row: Lodge, Fantham, Ellis, Craig, Finney.

Wednesday pictured in July 1965 after their summer break. They were to reach the FA Cup Final that season. Back row (left to right): Eustace, Hill, Hickton, Wicks, Mobley, Megson, Quinn. Front row: Smith, Dobson, Usher, Fantham, Finney, Young.

United had dropped to Division Two when this picture was taken in July 1969. They finished sixth in the table that season but were promoted the following season. Back row (left to right): John Short (coach), Addison, Hill, Colqhoun, Currie, Hodgkinson, Woodward, Hemsley, Powell, Harmston, Arthur Rowley (team manager). Front row: Badger, Buckley, Reece, Heaton, Tudor, Barlow, Salmons.

Action at Bramall Lane. With the cricket pavilion providing a backdrop, Billy Hodgson scores United's second goal in an October 1962 game against Bolton.

United Sixties favourite Mick Jones rises high to meet a corner from Alan Woodward in the match against Nottingham Forest in August 1967.

A break during a training session in December 1966 for United players (from left) Mick Hill, Alan Woodward, Mick Jones, Bernard Shaw and Len Badger.

Rotherham United's Second Division side at the start of the 1960-61 season. Back row (left to right): Houghton, Smith, Sawyer, Ironside, Waterhouse and Madden. Front row: Webster, Morgan, Kettleborough, Kirkman, Lambert and Perry.

Barnsley, then in the Third Division, pose for the camera before the start of the 1968-69 season. Back row (left to right): Pat Howard, John Bettany, Eric Brookes, Roy Ironside, Eric Winstanley, Bob Parker, Barry Murphy. Front row: John Hobson, Johnny Evans, Jimmy Robson, Alan Bradbury, George Hamstead.

Chesterfield's photocall at the start of the 1961-62 season. They were to finish 19th in the Fourth Division and it was the season Accrington Stanley resigned from the League. Back row (left to right): Holmes, Fowler, Whitham, Powell, Blakey, Poole, Broadhurst, Lovie. Centre row: Havenhand, Frear, Ord, Clarke, Kerry, Marshall, Rackstraw. Front: Lunn, Gissing, Sears.

Doncaster Rovers line up for the 1959-60 season. Back row (left to right), Makepeace, Darby, Mordue, Nimmo, Broadbent, Kilkenny, Gavin, Clark, Ardron (trainer), Staton, Wheatley, Swallow, Hymers, White, Fagan and Lunn. Front row:, Sharpe, Fernie, Leighton, Walker, Fletcher, Benson, Meredith, Bowskill and Cope.

Tears As The Owls Come Home From Wembley

The team coach leaves the Midland Station.

Police estimated that more than 100,000 turned out for Wednesday's homecoming, more than in 1935 when the Owls returned with the trophy.

Sheffield hadn't seen crowds like it for years. And the great swell of emotion that greeted Wednesday when they came home from Wembley in 1966 is still remembered by Owls fans as one of the most evocative experiences in the club's long history.

As one wise old Owl said as he joined in the wild enthusiasm outside the Town Hall: "I've been watching Wednesday for more than 60 years and I've never seen anything like this. It makes you wonder what the crowds would have been like had we won."

And when the team appeared on the balcony, the shout that went up from the massed crowds below could probably have been heard in Barnsley...

It was a heady mix of emotions – pride that the team had brought credit to Sheffield by battling its way to the final, sympathy for the players who had been so close to victory, and shock and disbelief that Everton, 2-0 down and struggling with just over half an hour to go, had snatched the glory with three goals in 15 minutes.

Wednesday's return to Sheffield was so moving that it made grown men cry. And many fans had also wept openly at the end of the game, particularly when the distraught players went on a lap of honour for their loyal but devastated followers.

"Ye Must Be Born Again" – religious fervour gets mixed up with Cup fervour as the team coach inches its way through the vast crowds.

The players and their wives arrive back from London. Captain Don Megson holds the Owls mascot.

A disappointed Johnny Fantham manages a smile on the way home from London.

Jim McCalliog's goal puts Wednesday ahead.

David Ford finds the net – and the Owls are two up.

His name will haunt Wednesday fans forever – Derek Temple's winner for Everton.

Defeated Wednesday go on a lap of honour.

Owls fans before the kick-off.

Skipper Don Megson carries out the introductions for Princess Margaret. Here she meets manager Alan Brown.

Up For The Cup!

South Yorkshire clubs had some amazing runs in the FA Cup during the Sixties.

United and Wednesday met in the quarter-finals in 1959-60, the Owls winning 2-0 but then losing to Blackburn in the semi-final.

Believe it or not, South Yorkshire had three teams in the last eight of the Cup in season 1960-61! Barnsley were beaten 2-1 by Leicester in a replay, Wednesday lost 2-0 to Burnley also in a replay and United carried the flag by beating Newcastle 3-1 to march into the semi-finals.

The Blades then lost 2-0 to Leicester in the semi-final in a second replay after two 0-0 draws.

In season 1961-62, United were in the last eight again, this time losing 0-1 to Burnley.

After reaching the final in 1966, Wednesday had another great cup run the following season. They reached the sixth round but went down 0-1 to Chelsea who had beaten United 2-0 in the previous round.

In 1967-68 it was United's turn to storm into the sixth round but they were beaten 1-0 by Leeds United.

Sheffield United in 1961 FA Cup semi-final action against Leicester. Keith Kettleborough rushes in to meet a ball from Billy Hodgson but Leicester full-back Norman heads clear.

Brave Dougie Loses Leg In Owls Coach Crash

It took a very special kind of courage from Dougie McMillan to pull Wednesday through one of the darkest days in their history when the Owls team coach crashed in Huntington on its way back from a game against Arsenal on Boxing Day 1960.

Inside-forward McMillan had to have his right leg amputated after the crash but won everyone's admiration for the way he battled back, rarely letting his spirits, or his sense of humour, flag.

Only 24 hours after the operation, he was lying in hospital at Huntington humming a pop song to himself. Doctors and nurses described him as "one of the bravest lads living."

Eight years later, Dougie, complete with fibre glass leg, actually played a competitive game for Hallam, the team he was managing part time. He decided to turn out in a Yorkshire League game against Hull Brunswick because of a shortage of players and played the full 90 minutes, wearing a track suit to cover his leg.

The wrecked Wednesday coach is taken away.

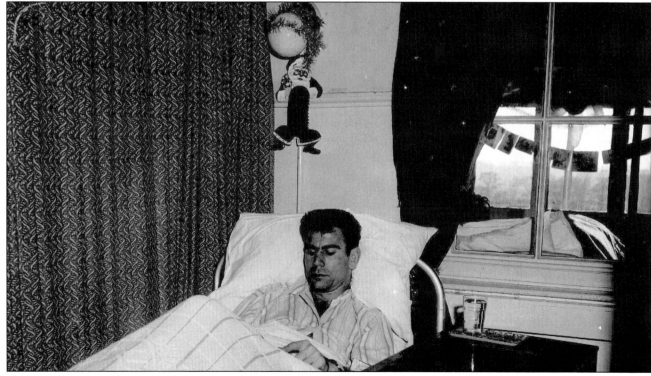

Dougie in hospital after losing his leg. Note the Santa dangling above his bed and the Christmas cards strung in the window.

Three weeks after the crash, Dougie was back at his beloved Hillsborough.

Dougie shakes hands with the players taking part in his benefit match on October 30 1961. It was a night of great emotion and no one would have been more sympathetic than Derek Dooley (far left) who had lost a leg through amputation in 1953.

The big kick-off. Dougie starts his benefit match under the watchful eye of referee George McCabe.

John and Sheila On Their Marks For A Fairytale Romance

It was the romance of the Sixties and the stuff of fairy tales when Sheffield long jumper Sheila Parkin met hurdler John Sherwood at the Tokyo Olympics in 1964 and married him in 1968.

And when Sheila won a silver medal in the 1968 Mexico Olympics and John a bronze in the hurdles, the best ever Olympic husband and wife achievement went straight into the record books.

Both of them also won gold medals in the 1970 Commonwealth Games and were awarded MBEs in 1975. It was a proud moment when the Queen told them: "It is not very often that I present awards to a husband and wife at the same time."

Pupils of Myers Grove Comprehensive, Sheffield, wave goodbye to popular PE teacher Sheila Sherwood as she sets off for the Mexico Olympics in 1968. She returned home in triumph, having won a silver medal in the long jump.

John and Sheila Sherwood catch up with The Star at the Mexico Olympics in 1968. The edition they are reading carried news of their successes and was mailed out to them by The Star's News Desk.

John and Sheila at Sheffield Midland Station with their Mexico medals.

The couple married in April 1968. Wishing them good luck is Sixties sprint queen, Dorothy Hyman.

Barnsley's Dorothy Is Queen Of The Track

Such was the modesty of sprinter Dorothy Hyman, a miner's daughter from Cudworth, Barnsley, that it was sometimes difficult to accept that she was the undisputed British queen of the track in the Sixties. Her devoted parents, dad Jack and mum Kathleen, gave her all the support they could but Dorothy had to work to finance her love of running and also relied on a group of loyal supporters to raise money for her running shoes.

Dorothy won silver and bronze medals in the 100 and 200 metres at the Rome Olympics in 1960 and a bronze in the relay in Tokyo in 1964. When her incredible career ended, she had picked up four gold, four silver, and three bronze medals in Olympic, European and Commonwealth competition.

In the early Seventies, a sports centre and all weather running track was opened in Cudworth and, fittingly, it was named after the girl who had brought so much honour to the small mining village.

Dorothy in 1963 with her collection of trophies and medals.

A huge crowd, including representatives from Cudworth Council, gathered around Dorothy's home in Bloemfontein Street, Cudworth, to welcome her home from the 1960 Rome Olympics where she won silver and bronze medals.

Dorothy training with another Barnsley sports star, Arthur Rowe, in 1962. Arthur was European, British Empire and British shot-putt champion in the early Sixties.

How'z that for a picture! Dorothy in training with Harold Bird in 1964, long before the world came to know him as Dickie the umpire.

Another picture of Arthur, taken in 1960. The Barnsley blacksmith's strength was such that he had a similar reputation to the biblical Samson. Feeding him was an expensive business – his average daily intake was six pints of milk, eight eggs, three big steaks, half a chicken and pounds of apples and oranges.

The Sixties Go Swimmingly For Jill

Swimmer Jill Slattery, from Norton, Sheffield, was captain of the British women's team at the 1968 Mexico Olympics and holder of British breaststroke records over 100 and 200 metres.

She took fifth place at the Tokyo Olympics in 1964 and won a gold and silver medal at the Jamaican Commonwealth Games in 1966.

When her competition days were over, Jill moved to America and became coach of the Indianapolis Athletic Club swimming team.

Jill Slattery (left) proudly shows off her silver medal from the 110-yard breastroke final in the 1966 Jamaican Commonwealth Games. England team colleague Diane Harris (right) pipped Jill by one tenth of a second to take the gold.

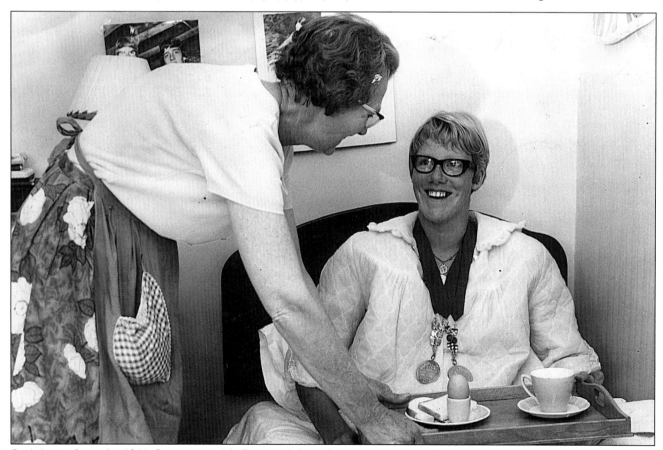

Back home from the 1966 Commonwealth Games, it's breakfast in bed for Jill, still wearing her gold and silver medals.

Jill in action in 1967.

Rotherham Miler Alan Fast-Tracks His Way to Fame

Alan Simpson from Rotherham was Britain's outstanding miler for several years in the Sixties and smashed the four-minute barrier no less than 11 times.

He also broke Derek Ibbotson's mile record in 1965 and a year earlier missed out on a medal by a whisker in the Tokyo Olympics.

With 80 yards to go, Simpson was lying second behind Peter Snell, ten metres clear of the third place runner. But a few metres from the tape his legs buckled and he missed out on a medal.

Eager to give something back to running after his retirement, Alan trained Rotherham runner Denise Creamer who won the British women's 800 metres title in 1975.

A winner again! A mud-splattered Alan breasts the tape in 1964. The venue is unknown but it could be Millmoor football ground because the cheering crowd look very much like Rotherham United supporters.

Glory for Rotherham's Alan Simpson as he wins the 1500 metres for Britain against Poland at the White City in 1965.

The *Sheffield Telegraph* and *Star* honoured local athletes competing in the 1964 Tokyo Olympics by making special presentations to them. Left to right are: Jill Slattery, Michael Finley (Editor of the *Sheffield Telegraph*), Dorothy Hyman, Alan Simpson, Tom Watson (Editor of *The Star*) and Sheila Sherwood (then Sheila Parkin).

Yorkshire – and Boycott – Dominate The Sixties

During an incredible decade, Yorkshire won the County Championship no fewer than six times, in 1960, 62, 63, 66, 67 and 68.

Yet there must have been a few cricket sages among the Yorkshire membership who wondered what the future held when the legendary Len Hutton retired in 1960.

But coming through the ranks was an ambitious youngster from Barnsley who made it quite clear that he wasn't prepared to let the grass grow under his feet.

He scored his first 100 for Yorkshire Seconds at Bridlington in August 1961 and made his first team debut against Pakistan at Bradford in June 1962.

Geoff Boycott had arrived and, fittingly, his first Roses century (145 not out) was in Sheffield at Bramall Lane in June 1963.

The rest is history and rich history at that. He went on to captain Yorkshire and England and scored more than 40,000 runs in first-class cricket, including 151 centuries.

His 100th century was on Yorkshire soil, for England against Australia at Headingley in 1977, and in the 22,000 crowd was another history maker- Len Hutton, one of the few other batsmen to have notched a ton of tons.

As well as their County Championship triumphs, Yorkshire also won the Gillette Cup in 1965 and 1969. The Sixties decade was also memorable for other Yorkshire records.

Wicketkeeper Jimmy Binks had the most dismissals in a season, 107, in 1960 (96 caught and 11 stumped) and Phil Sharpe took the most catches in a season, 70, in 1962. This equalled Tunnicliffe's 70 in 1901.

And in January 1963, Yorkshire, founded at a meeting at the Adelphi Hotel, Sheffield, in 1863, celebrated their centenary.

There was just one record in the Sixties the county will want to forget. On 20 May 1965, Yorkshire were dismissed for just 23 by Hampshire at Middlesborough.

Yorkshire, county champions in 1960. Back row (from left): Stott, Taylor, Cowan, D. Wilson, Binks, Padgett. Front (from left): Bolus, Trueman, J.V. Wilson (captain), Close, Illingworth, Hatton.

Chatting before net practice in 1965
are (from left) Chris Balderstone,
Geoff Hodgson and Geoff Boycott.

Something of an historic picture, this – Fred Trueman playing a DEFENSIVE shot to a ball from Lancashire's Brian Statham in August 1961.

Heartbreak For Heart-throb Roger

Sheffield's Roger Taylor was Britain's number one tennis player in the middle and late Sixties.

His good looks gave him a film star following which reached fever pitch in 1967 when he battled through to the semi-finals at Wimbledon, the first British player to get to that stage since Mike Sangster in 1961.

It ended in heartbreak for heart throb Roger, beaten in a five-set game by Germany's Wilhelm Bungert after being 2-1 up.

Roger, who went on to run a tennis centre in the Algarve region of Portugal when his competitive days were over, also reached the semi-finals at Wimbledon in 1970 and 1973.

One of the highlights of his career was knocking champion Rod Laver out of Wimbledon in 1970.

Roger with his mum in 1962.

What a racket! Roger leaving London to play in Australia in 1968.

World Cup – Willkommen Says Sheffield

Sheffield had its first real taste of life continental style when the city was chosen to host some of the 1966 World Cup matches.

Pubs were allowed to stay open later for foreign visitors and working men's clubs provided late-night cabaret.

Foreign flags fluttered from poles all over Sheffield as a welcome to the fans who came to support their countries and the different languages heard in shops, restaurants and pubs gave the city a cosmopolitan atmosphere.

On the field, West Germany thrashed Switzerland 5-0 in Sheffield's opening match, went on to beat Uruguay 4-0 in the quarter-final at Hillsborough and then lost to England 4-2 in the final.

World Cup flags outside Sheffield's Midland Station.

This Guinness Time Clock was erected in Fitzalan Square, Sheffield, as part of the World Cup celebrations.

The BBC's World Cup commentary team (back row, left to right): Frank Bough, Alan Weeks, David Coleman and Wally Barnes. Front row, left to right: Ken Aston, Kenneth "they think it's all over, it is now" Wolstenholme and Arthur Ellis.

A German supporter tries to run on to the pitch at the West Germany-Uruguay quarter-final at Hillsborough but is put back behind the wall by police.

Members of Sheffield's World Cup Liaison Committee pose in their special World Cup suits. From left to right at Hillsborough are: Dr Andrew Stephen (chairman of Sheffield Wednesday FC), Harold Shentall (chairman of the committee), Ernest Kangley (committee secretary) and Eric Taylor (secretary and general manager of Sheffield Wednesday FC).